Dare to Say ... "Yes"

It Happened on an Island

... It Could Happen to You

LeEllen Bubar

Scripture taken from the King James Version of the Bible.

WestBow Press books may be ordered through booksellers or by contacting:

WestBow Press
A Division of Thomas Nelson & Zondervan
1663 Liberty Drive
Bloomington, IN 47403
www.westbowpress.com
1 (866) 928-1240

ISBN: 978-1-9736-0685-7 (sc)
ISBN: 978-1-9736-0686-4 (hc)
ISBN: 978-1-9736-0684-0 (e)

Library of Congress Control Number: 2017916104

Print information available on the last page.

WestBow Press rev. date: 01/24/2018

Contents

"If you want one year of prosperity, grow grain. If you want ten years of prosperity, grow trees. If you want one hundred years of prosperity, grow people."

—Chinese Proverb

The following true stores are about people who dared to say, "Yes, God."

Clif and LeEllen Bubar said, "Yes, God, we will serve you on St. Croix Island." Some pictures of those who said yes; read about the following true stores of some who said, "Yes, God." Our Father's blessing on these who do.

Foreword

Dare to Say Yes

**Having faith isn't easy.
It's not easy when overwhelming circumstances bombard us in life.**

It's not easy when we can't see a way out. It takes faith. Faith means believing in something we can't see.

God doesn't tell us to believe in Him because we can see what will happen. God tells us to believe in Him because we can't know the future – but He does, and He wants us to trust in Him. This is just what happened in the life of the author of this book. God caused them to take a big step of faith, and they dared to say yes. And because they did, many, many others did, as you will learn as you read through the pages. Many lives were changed forever, and new churches were planted, souls were transformed. I could tell you about our story, but I'm sure you will find it in this book much better told than I could.

Their lives haven't always been easy; in fact, I know that they had many trials; because of a strong faith in God of the Bible, the God Who called them and challenged them to dare to say yes, they have had a great time of rejoicing in Him and received multiple blessings from Him.

I urge you to read this book, and maybe you too will dare to say yes to God. Ludvig Jahansen Jr.

Ludvig Johansen, Jr. (better known as Sonny; he dared to say yes by serving as the deacon and song leader; he also used his bulldozer to prepare the land his parents gave us to build a Baptist church)

Preface

The purpose of LeEllen Bubar's book *Dare to Say Yes* is to challenge, interest, and inspire people of all ages and all walks of life: college students, grandchildren, young people, and seniors; it will make you think about the Great Commission. It is one of the great responsibilities Jesus left for Christians to carry out. Bookstores have shelves of books on romance, family planning, sex, grandparenting, homeschooling, and much more. Books on missions are usually tucked away on an unnoticed shelf.

There seems to be a decline in long-term career missionaries, while the number of short-termers has increased. In 2009, Pastor Joy, of Bethel Baptist Church, Bradenton, Florida, sponsored a team of twenty-eight adults and youth to work on mission projects on St. Croix. Members of the team painted and worked on the interior of the building in connection with the Light House, a mission of the Southgate Baptist Church, where Pastor and Mrs. McCulla minister. Others shared Christ and gave tracts to street people who gathered after having breakfast at the Light House. In the evenings, the team helped with daily vacation Bible school at Southgate Baptist Church. The team stayed at the Christian school building at the Sunny Isle Baptist Church, where Pastor and Mrs. Gardner minister. Short-term missions have had a great effect on home churches and mission churches. They raise missionary career interest among the youth and stretch faith and causes growth and an open mind to a part of God's world, in this case, an island, St. Croix.

When Clif and I were students at Trinity College, we were challenged about missions; at our home church in Bradenton, Florida, we heard messages on the Great Commission: "Go ye into all the world and preach the gospel to every creature" and "Why should some people hear the gospel twice when some haven't heard it once?"

A plea was given: "Who will go?" Clif and I were soon to graduate from Trinity College. We had a desire to serve the Lord, but up to this point, we didn't know where.

After the service, we decided to talk to Don Luttrell, the missionary. He had flown a Cessna 172 down through the Caribbean islands, looking for an island to start a Christian radio station. He told us about St. Croix, one of the US Virgin Islands, where there were no Baptist churches; the Crucian people spoke English. It was a primitive island in that day, with donkeys and donkey carts and a very few cars.

We said, "We'll go." Our faith was greater than the unforeseen step we had taken to go to an island we knew little about. We couldn't foresee what was around the corner. Our step of faith put our lives on the line. Taking hold of God's promises correlated with our faith: "Now faith is the substance of things hoped for, the evidence of things not seen" (Hebrews 11:1).

Clif and I graduated from Trinity College on May 16, 1956, and five months later, on October 1, Don Luttrell met us in Puerto Rico and flew us to the island of St.

Croix. God blessed us as we spent the next thirty-six years planting Baptist churches on the island.

If readers are encouraged to dare to say, "Yes, God, I'll go. I'll serve you, wherever you lead me," then this book will have accomplished its mission.

Acknowledgments

I want to thank God for calling us to a life worth living and for writing all these special moments on the pages of our lives, with so many special people in each chapter.

My special thanks and appreciation goes to all of our friends who encouraged me to write a book about the Lord's work on St. Croix.

Sonny and Sarah Johansen were members of the Frederiksted Baptist Church in the early 1960s, soon after Clif and I founded and established the church on St. Croix. The Johansens greatly encouraged me to write a book. The title *Dare to Say Yes* was suggested by Henry Erickson, husband of my niece, Nancy Lyons.

Naomi Knepper, a longtime friend and former English teacher used her expertise editing stories. Naomi wanted the missionary's mind and heart to run through the book from cover to cover. Now with our Lord, Naomi wasn't able to complete the task, but my wonderful granddaughter, Shelley Bubar, one of the top students in her class, helped on the project.

God supplied Bonita Files. She has been such a blessing at just the right time to keep the project going from proofreading, typing, and making the right connections for WestBow Press. Praise the Lord, thank you, thank you Bonita Files.

Another woman helped Naomi and Bonita with typing and formatting this document and making it ready for publishing: Jaya Milam also assisted in editing at the end. Our Lord sent these ladies to me at just the right time to keep this project moving forward.

Also, a special thank you to Alexis D'Orsi for providing us resources during the editing sessions of this book.

Brenda Southerland was a blessing as she helped with Bible scriptures that went with each of the stories in the book.

Cynthia and Claude Ashby, active members of the Sunny Isle Baptist Church on St. Croix, were helpful with computer research for copyright materials and also helped with some typing.

Thank you to Gwen Carmichael, retired educator, Dixie County School System in Florida, for assisting in editing the book.

A very special thanks to Dr. Rick Amato, evangelist and president of Rick Amato Ministries, a graduate of Liberty University; he was a speaker at Southgate and Sunny Isle Baptist Churches on St. Croix, and he urged me to write a book about our ministry. He wrote a letter on behalf of this book to Thomas Nelson Publishers: "Thank God you finally decided to capture the historic work that you and Clifford pioneered on St. Croix … how thankful I am that you have decided to write *Dare to Say Yes!* … this will ensure that the miracles the Lord has done will not be forgotten."

We greatly appreciated Johnathan Eusebe's efforts as our music director in leading the worship services. We really enjoyed his beautiful voice and his outstanding Christian personality.

Clif and I dared to say, "Yes, God, we'll serve you," and we have never been sorry. Many thanks to all who encouraged me to write this book about our lifetime of service to our Lord and how God led us to start the Lord's work on St. Croix Island where there were no Baptist Churches.

Introduction

History is the record of what people in the past have done. This is a record of an adventurous missionary journey. It captures the historic work that Clifford and LeEllen Bubar pioneered on St. Croix: how the first Baptist church came about on the island.

Clifford built the first Baptist church in the town of Frederiksted. Later, property was given to build another church in the Sunny Isle area, making a sister Baptist church on St. Croix.

In the meantime, a Spanish couple came to know the Lord as their Savior. We studied the Bible with them. They also attended the Frederiksted Baptist Church and brought Spanish friends with them; although not understanding much English, they were faithful to services. God led them to purchase a piece of land to build a church for their Spanish-speaking people; at the time, Ping was operating a bulldozer for a company in St. Croix. After leading their parents to the Lord, they built a church. Ping and his son Jose studied a Bible course through the mail from Costa Rica. Ping was ordained and became the pastor of the Spanish church. He preached in Spanish for the Spanish-speaking congregation.

They dared to say yes, and God has blessed them.

Also, the youth were on the hearts of the Bubars. Carib Camp was founded in the hills of Spart Hall. The camp was built in the hills of Creeky Damn Road, Frederiksted, on the side of a hill where Bible stories were shared with twenty-five youth during the summer. Swimming in the Caribbean, ball on the side of the hill, and crafts were all a part of Carib Youth Camp in the summer. Carib Youth Camp filled our summers, helping to reach children and the youth, along with their parents. Later, Ludvig Johansen gave us another beautiful piece of land east of Christiansted, overlooking the beautiful Caribbean Sea, and a third church was built there. We had a share in leading Ludvig and Mrs. Johansen to the Lord, along with Sonny, their son. Praises and thanks to the Lord.

You will read heart-felt, inspiring stories of how God's awesome love and direction led the Bubars (also known at Trinity College as Kip and Lee).

Early in their ministry, the Bubars visited people in the villages and towns on the island of St. Croix. They acquainted themselves with people as they went door-to-door, enrolling people in home Bible studies.

They usually met the Crucian women in the daytime; usually grandmas were home taking care of their grandchildren. A typical grandma would come to the door with a colorful apron over her dress and a babushka on her head, and a straw hat on top of the babushka. They thus kept the sun and heat off their heads.

Some women worked as maids. Others were nurses at the hospital. Some were doctors. In fact, a black lady doctor delivered our baby Mark at the clinic in Frederiksted.

Some of the men fished by casting a net, like Peter in the Bible, or throwing a line. Some worked in the cane fields cutting sugar cane, while others worked at the factory where Cruzan rum was made (and still is). Others drove taxi cars and buses. Both men and women were postal workers. Some were attorneys.

While the Bubars were witnessing and introducing people to Jesus through Bible studies, bridges were being built and ground work was being laid. People were drawn to Christians with a caring heart before being drawn to Christ. Clif used a hammer and saw as a need arose for a closet or shelf in a humble dwelling place, where clothes were hung on nails. LeEllen was handy with a paint brush and a bucket of paint.

Sometimes, Clif and LeEllen took turns at night sitting with a sick member of a family in the hospital, relieving the family of long tiring hours. Love and concern involved them in helping people. It bridged the way to share Christ with them. One of the greatest expressions of love for an individual is the desire to see them find Jesus Christ as their Savior. There were many opportunities to witness and to lead people to Christ, and it all happened on an island … it could happen to you.

This book was written to ensure that the miracles the Lord has done will not be forgotten.

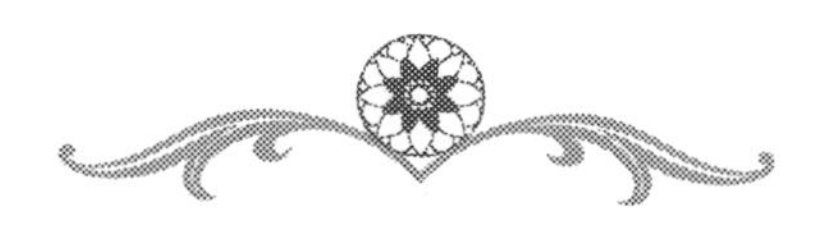

Our World, the Island of St. Croix

Ye have not chosen me, but I have chosen you, that ye should go and bring forth fruit, and that your fruit should remain.

—John 15:16

Jesus said, "Go ye into all the world, and preach the gospel to every creature." One might ask, "How could you possibly go into all the world and preach the gospel?" My sister, Nadyne, and her husband, Abe Miller, went to Japan as missionaries. As for Clif and me, our world was rather small; it was the island of St. Croix.

In 1956, God sent us as missionaries to St. Croix in the Caribbean. There were no Baptist churches on the island, and we discovered that St. Croix would be a place to pioneer a new work for the Lord. God laid church planting on our hearts, but really our work was the people of the island. The people of St. Croix are known as Crucians, and it was for them that we went to the island. Like humanity all over the globe, they have great spiritual needs.

So what is so special about this island where we spent our lives? Well, let me tell you a little about it: In 1917,

President Woodrow Wilson led the United States in the purchase of the three Virgin Islands to use as protection for the Panama Canal. The purchase price of twenty-five million dollars amounted to $295 per acre. For that day, it was quite a price when you think that Alaska was purchased for five cents per acre.

Many years ago, the island was known as Santa Crux, St. Croix, meaning Saint Cross. Sugar cane fields were everywhere; the sugar cane factory was centrally located in Estate Bethlehem. Many of the sugar cane fields have now been replaced with new housing developments. The sugar factory has been sold and moved off the island. For many years, rum was the main product of the island. It still is, now made from syrup imported from other islands. Even though it is part of the economy, it is a serious problem.

Large Company, built in the 1960s, was one of the biggest firms in the world and provided work for people on St. Croix before it closed. Cruise ships bring tourists, which are welcome and help the economy. The climate is a main attraction, moderate and extremely pleasant, seldom varying from the normal temperatures of 70 to 80 degrees. Luxury hotels, both new and old, can be found near the beaches and in towns.

St. Croix is two and a half hours flying time from Miami, and there are direct flights from New York. Many people have moved to St. Croix from the States and other areas, and the influx has affected land values. Driving on the left-hand side of the road in cars designed to drive on the right is an adventure. In fact, when you're behind the wheel, remember a St. Croix slogan: "Think Left."

The Danish décor of many shops in the towns of

Christiansted and Frederiksted make them unique and remind us of the history of the island.

The land is tillable, which makes St. Croix different from some of the other islands in the area. Most of the one hundred islands in the Caribbean are just rock, but St. Croix has cattle and lovely gardens. Between Christiansted and Frederiksted lies the St. George Village Botanical Gardens. They cover sixteen acres and contain ruins of the nineteenth century.

There are two distinct towns on St. Croix: Frederiksted and Christiansted. We love St. Croix.

While the physical attractions of the island are splendid, our world is the people who live there. We're proud to identify with the people. They are the reason we came. Like humanity all over the globe, these people have great spiritual needs. When we first came, we saw fishermen who still fished by casting a net, like Peter in the Bible, or by throwing lines. Other people worked in the cane fields cutting sugar cane, while others worked in the sugar factory and still others at the factory where Cruzan rum is made. Others drove taxi cars and buses, were attorneys, worked in the post office, or could be seen with donkey carts.

Some of the women worked as maids; others were teachers in public schools or nurses and doctors at the hospitals. The older women of the island wore colorful aprons over their dresses, a babushka on their head, and then a straw hat on top of that in an effort to keep the sun and heat out.

We're happy to count many of the Crucians among our dearest friends and loved ones. But the devil didn't love St. Croix; he tried to hinder our work. The Bible says he is like a roaring lion seeking whom he may devour. But he went hungry on the days I'm about to tell you about. Yes, for thirty-six years, our world was an island, the beautiful St. Croix.

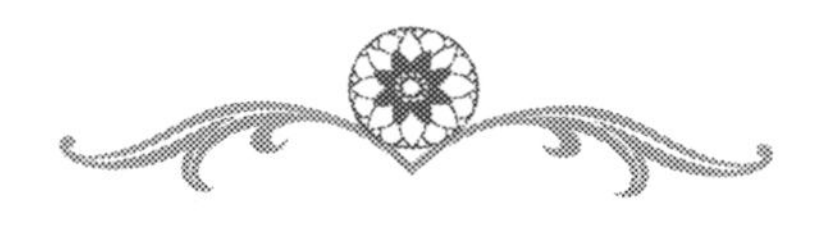

Some Good Advice, after All

"For my thoughts are not your thoughts, neither are your ways my ways," saith the Lord. "As the heavens are higher than the earth, so are my ways higher than your ways and my thoughts than your thoughts."

—Isaiah 55:8–9

I remember getting some good advice when I was a young girl. I had been living my life, just flowing along with no purpose in mind. My sister, Nadyne, was a graduate of Moody Bible Institute in Chicago and was preparing to be a missionary to Japan. She was giving some good last-minute advice to her younger sister before leaving.

She said, "Attend Trinity Bible College for at least one year, and it will give you direction for your life. Studying the Bible won't hurt anyone. It will make you a better Christian. It will make you a better wife when married, and a better mother if you have children." Then she added, "Maybe God would want you to be a missionary someday."

I rejected the idea as I went on my way to work, saying, "I had enough studying in school. God doesn't want all of us to missionaries." But a smile came across my face, and I added, "You be the missionary, and I will help support you."

We have a plaque on our wall that reads: "If you want God to laugh, make your own plans." You will be surprised what God has in store for you as you surrender to His Lordship.

For me, I ended up following Nadyne's inspired advice and went to Trinity College, and later, I became a missionary. God knows best, always.

College Sweethearts

For I know the thoughts that I think toward
you saith the Lord, thoughts of peace not
of evil, to give you an expected end.

—Jeremiah 29:11

The idea of going off to Trinity College scared me. However, my pastor's wife encouraged me by reminding me that God had good plans for me and that they didn't include harm. In fact, He planned to give me hope and a future. The certainty of God's Word helped me to risk the uncertainties of the unknowns concerning college. As it turned out, college was a blast. I attended parties, actually won a prize for the funniest costume and clown act, sang in a girl's trio, and attended all kinds of Christian activities, fellowships, and Bible classes. Growing in the Lord was so much fun. I also met my sweetheart at college, but I'm getting a little ahead of my story.

This part of the story takes place at Trinity Bible College, at that time located in Clearwater, Florida. Dr. W. T. Watson purchased a hotel that had been a gambling casino, and with God's help, he was able to transform it into a fine college. No longer would people risk their money for uncertain gain on those grounds; now, they could risk their very lives to a God Who had good and certain plans for them. Instead of loss, all who set foot on the property would experience great gain, growing in the grace and knowledge of God and in His vision and purpose for their lives.

It is said that when Billy Graham was a student at Trinity College, he practiced preaching his sermons to the trees instead of to a congregation. Could it be the trees joyfully heard and praised God as Billy preached the Word? The Bible tells us that if the people won't praise God, other creations of God will. In Isaiah 55, it actually tells us that the "trees of the field will clap their hands."

There was another man, Clifford Bubar, who also attended Trinity. Kip was tall, handsome, shy, and soft-spoken. Although he was a quiet man, he sure could make the trumpet talk. He was in the Trinity Trumpet Trio, an amazing group to hear. All the girls at Trinity noticed Kip, including me.

Kip was born in Maine. People born in Maine and who stay in Maine are called "Maine'ers," but if they leave Maine, they are called "Mainiacs." Kip became a Mainiac when Dr. Watson visited Kip's home church and challenged young men and women to travel to Florida to study at Trinity College. Kip took the challenge of his life and has never been the same.

When Kip said yes to God's plans for his life, he had no way of knowing that he would be meeting me – a girl born in Lansing, Michigan, now from Bradenton, Florida –at Trinity College in Clearwater.

All that to say, God can get you where you need to be; just trust Him and follow His leading. He'll get you to the right place at the right time. He's good at that.

One day as I was going to class, Kip said to me, "Lee, how about a date Friday night?"

I said, "I'll check in my little date book and let you know."

After all, my mother had always told me, "Never chase a boy, and don't let him think that you are too anxious." But then I worried that Kip might be too shy to follow up with me and ask for an answer. He didn't get disappointed; he was back the next day for my answer, and I accepted.

On our first date, we attended a missionary meeting in the chapel, the former gambling room where a roulette wheel was used by multimillionaires and was automatically lowered through the floor when surprise police raids took place. Sunday Vesper services were now held in the room, and the roulette wheel had been put to better use, as an offering plate. It's funny how God can change the nature of things and people. He delights in doing that.

After the missionary meeting, we joined other couples in the Rainbow Room, which had been converted into a dating parlor. Couples could play games and have refreshments while chaperones kept a watchful eye on everything. During casino days, the Rainbow Room had been a dance hall with colored lights and a bar.

Kip was shy and quiet, and so he prodded me to keep talking every time there was a lull in our conversation. I talked about my parents, my brothers, my missionary sister and her husband, my aunts, uncles, cousins, and even my dog, Pupsie. He knew my whole family at the end of our first date.

Our dates continued. It was also pretty neat that we had chosen some of the same electives before we knew each other. We were both in the same prayer group, Islands of the Sea, where we prayed for missionaries, and we had both chosen a child evangelism class. Our mission's teacher stirred our hearts and minds toward missions. We were active in the tract club ministry, where we gave out tracts in the community. We were in special music groups, and sang and traveled with the choir. All of this was part of a bigger plan God had for our lives, and we began to understand our purpose.

I think it was love at first sight between the two of us. Even my mother said it looked like love, and when I asked her how she knew, she said, "I can tell by the way you look at each other."

I'm glad it went deeper than that, though. Our love had grown for each other and for the Lord. After Kip and I had dated for about a year, he asked my father for my hand in marriage and showed him the beautiful diamond ring that he had worked so hard to get for me. My dad knew that Kip was made of good stuff, because he had worked for him in a gas station and had proved that he was a good worker and that he would be a good husband and provider. That was important to my dad. He gave his permission.

Afterwards, Kip felt it would be proper to ask Dr. Watson to get his approval regarding giving me the engagement ring while we were students at the school. I wondered how Kip would get the courage up to ask, because he was so shy at the time. Dr. Watson had clearly stated in chapel that Trinity College was not a match box and that students were there to study, not find mates.

As it turned out, Dr. Watson appreciated Kip's respect for the authority of the college and told him that he could give me the ring, but that I couldn't wear it as it might start a fad with other students who were less serious about their relationship. While Kip appreciated the wisdom of this, he told Dr. Watson that he wanted it known that I belonged to him, and he wanted me to wear the ring. Dr. Watson said he would take it before the board members. Several weeks passed, and Kip went back to follow up with him. By this time, sure enough, there were five other couples waiting for ring confirmation. Dr. Watson was pretty wise about students and fads.

One day, Dr. Watson called all the couples in his office, along with a member of the board. He told us that it was voted that students could be engaged but would receive no extra privileges. It was near Christmastime, and Kip and I finally became engaged, as did the five other couples. However, after graduation, all the other couples broke up and gave the rings back.

Trinity had rules for couples. We could talk no longer than three minutes at a time on our way to class or on campus, so some conversations were finished by writing notes. I want to share two of our Trinity "sweetheart notes" with you. They are the beginning of what was not to be a fad for us, but the start of a marriage still going strong for over sixty-two years.

On May 22, 1954, we made a promise to each other and to the Lord. Rev. D. E. Luttrell, our pastor at Calvary Baptist Church in Bradenton, performed our marriage ceremony

Kip wrote:

> Dearest Wife to Be,
>
> Only 173 days for 4,132 hours before May 22, 1954 at 2pm. Darling Lee, I must write

a note to my one and only sweetheart. Darling, I asked God to give the girl that He wanted me to have. Lee, you are the one, I know for sure. I believe God wants us to live for Him and work for Him together. I have given you the ring with my whole heart, for life, Lee. We'll be happy, God is with us. Everything we have belongs to Him. God is so good. Let's love Him first and then our love for each other will be complete. I feel like God is doing a great work in our hearts. Lee dear, pray much, know that I love only you. With my whole heart I say, "God bless you, Lee." Darling, I love you so much. Isaiah 40:31

All my love, Kip

I wrote back to Kip:

My Kip Honey,

You are so sweet. Thanks for your note. I could feel the Lord all through it. I know you are so happy, and I am too! The Lord has filled us with His joy. Kip, I feel so close to you and through the fellowship we've had with the Lord, I know we have been drawn closer to Him. He must be pleased that we involve Him in our conversations and in our notes. I'm so glad we love the Lord. I'm His and you're His. You are so precious to me and I love you so much.

Kip, I'll always love you, Lee

The love God gave us for each other lasted longer than a fad, so not long after graduation, wedding bells rang for us. On Saturday, May 22, at 2:00 p.m., Kip and I were married by Dr. D. E. Luttrell at the church where we were members, Calvary Baptist in Bradenton, Florida. We were honored to have Dr. Watson, the president of Trinity College, in attendance (even though we guessed he was still maintaining his assertion that Trinity College was not a "match box"). Many friends attended our wedding, and we had our honeymoon in a log cabin by the river. I remember that Kip and I attended a little Baptist church the next morning, and when the preacher heard that we were newlyweds, he said from the pulpit, "God bless you both for coming here this morning."

After our wedding, we helped at a Christian youth camp at the Suwanee River in Branford and then returned to Trinity College in September to study for another year as a married couple. We graduated with a four-year BA degree. God called us to be missionaries in St. Croix, one of the Virgin Islands in the Caribbean where we served for thirty-six years, planting churches.

Don't be afraid to say yes to God and take a bold step forward, regardless of where you're at in life, whether it's making a decision to attend a Bible college or rededicating your life wholeheartedly to the Lord. He has a purpose and a plan for your life, and He is waiting for you to dare to say yes to Him. Life unfolds as you walk with Him. Your story won't look exactly like ours, but then again, it's not supposed to.

Also, if you're single and praying for a godly mate,

don't settle for anything less. There is so much pressure today to lower your standards and to disobey God just to win the love of a person. God has better for you than that. If God can't trust a person, you can't either. Dare to ask *and trust* God for a godly mate, one that won't ask you to exchange the future God has for you for one of regrets. A godly mate is worth the wait, and when you honor God in all of your decisions, He will honor you. Dare to trust God, even with your heart and your most precious dreams.

Clif and LeEllen Bubar, Trinity College sweethearts

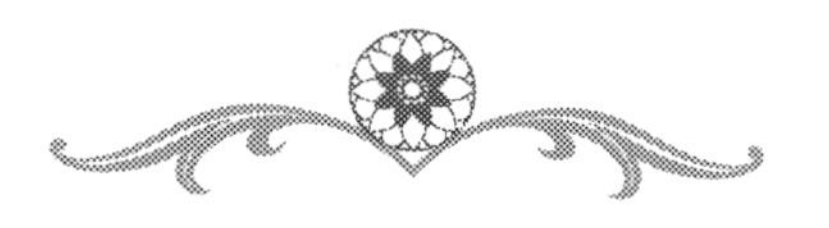

Camp: God's Preparation

For we are his workmanship, created in Christ
Jesus unto good works which God hath before
ordained that we should walk in them.

—Ephesians 2:10

While attending Trinity College, Kip and I had the opportunity to help at a Christian youth camp one summer. The camp was on the Suwannee River in Florida. We and other Trinity students were involved in helping to get the camp ready for the summer youth groups. Some of the tasks included cleaning and cutting and trimming trees. Sometimes, snakes shot out of their nests when brush and debris were being burnt. The Trinity fellows would quickly seize the snakes, or anything else they could catch on the end of their rakes, to chase the girls with and make them squeal. It was all good natured and broke up some of the monotony of our chores.

One day, when I was driving back to camp from town, I ran over a huge rattlesnake with six rattles; it was in the middle of the road when my car ran over it. Make sure it was dead, I picked it up with a stick and put it in the car. The Bible tells us we reap what we sow, and it was indeed time to reciprocate some of the same kind of mischief the Trinity fellows were known for

I drove back to camp where the guys were working. I quietly got Kip's attention, and he helped me unload the large dead rattlesnake from the trunk. We coiled the snake in front of the kitchen door with all six rattles showing, so it looked like it was ready to strike. The men had taken a break from working to come into the kitchen area to get a drink of water, at which point I couldn't resist yelling, "Rattlesnake! Rattlesnake! There's a snake by the kitchen door!"

Sure enough, all the guys mobilized and came running, armed with shovels, rakes, picks, and even a gun to shoot the rattlesnake. They worked feverishly to kill the already-dead snake. Imagine their surprise.

I have to admit that I took a great deal of joy watching them fall for this trick wholeheartedly. I can still see the expressions on their faces when they realized that they had been tricked. Note: A good sense of humor always comes in handy, whether you're working Stateside or overseas on a mission. Ministry can be fun.

The snake pranks mysteriously stopped after the rattlesnake incident and the camp cleanup work was completed. Soon, the youth arrived for camp. Clif volunteered to be the handyman, and I was the camp nurse. That summer, we gained valuable experience and blessings as we took part in various camp activities. We didn't know it at the time, but God was already preparing us to be able to start Carib Camp, one of the first Christian youth ministries on St. Croix. He also showed us that a good sense of humor is something to include on the packing list when heading off to the mission field. It comes in handy … often.

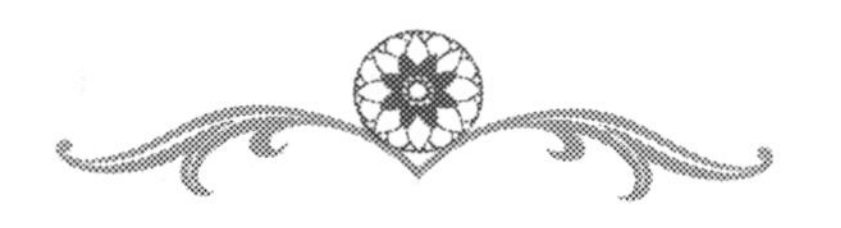

Answering the Call

Let them give glory unto the Lord and
declare his praise in the islands.
—Isaiah 42:12

The year was 1956. Don Luttrell had just come back from flying his single-engine airplane through the Caribbean islands in search of an island to build a Christian radio station. Don was speaking at Calvary Baptist Church in Bradenton, Florida, and telling us that he had located an island, Vieques, Puerto Rico. While searching for an island, he had also landed on St. Croix, a US Virgin Island. At the time, St. Croix was very primitive with donkeys and donkey carts everywhere, very few cars, and absolutely no Baptist churches. We learned that the people there were called Crucians and that they spoke English a Crucian dialect. Our interest was stirred! Don spoke that night of the Great Commission, quoting Mark 16:15: "Go ye into all the world and preach the gospel to every creature." We remember him asking, "Why should some people hear the gospel twice when some haven't even heard it once?" We were touched, and our hearts were stirred. An invitation was given: "Who will go?"

We already knew our answer. Clif and I were just about ready to graduate from Trinity with our BA degrees when we heard Don speak, and we were eager to serve the Lord as missionaries; we just weren't sure where. We decided, "Let's talk to Don; if it's His will, God will bring it to pass."

Of course, it was God's will for us to proclaim His praise to an island. He had been waiting for willing servants who would trust Him enough to step out of their comfort zones and into His care, where the action was. Some people complain about God's timing being slow, but we found that once we dared to say yes to God and to his vision for St. Croix, His timing was brisk, and all the right doors just seemed to fly open.

With our vision now firmly fixed before us, we finished up our exams and graduated with bachelor's degrees from Trinity. Our next step was to raise missionary support and pack up and head for St. Croix. Don introduced us to Pastor Guy Rainwater at Eastside Baptist Church in Atlanta. We gave testimonies at the church; Clif and I sang a duet, and Don and Clif played their trumpets. The church voted to support us for $200 a month and to send us to St. Croix as their missionaries. What a whirlwind; it happened so quickly. But then something else happened quickly and unexpectedly as well.

Answering the call; dare to say yes.

Dare to Say Yes

Trust in the Lord with all thine heart; and
lean not unto thine own understanding.
—Proverbs 3:5

At every turn in life, we decide whether we trust God with everything we have: our lives, our future, our relationships, our loved ones, our finances, and our dreams. It's not so hard to trust God when things are going great, but in times of setbacks, we surely cannot afford to drop our faith and begin to doubt our God. We need to be so committed to trusting God that we can be like Job, who in the midst of extreme devastation and physical affliction, resolutely declared of God, "Though He slay me, yet will I trust in Him" (Job 13:15).

My older sister, Nadyne, had attended Moody Bible Institute and Wheaton College, studying to be a missionary. Nadyne was determined to sell all out to God, and she did. China was very tough to get into at the time and remained a closed door for Nadyne, but not one to throw in the towel, she and her husband, Abe, went as missionaries to Japan instead. After Nadyne and Abe had been in Japan for over three years, the Lord provided a way for my parents to go to see her; they took a cruise ship to finally reunite with their daughter. While the ship was making its way to Japan with my parents aboard, they received the most horrible news: Nadyne had been bitten by a mosquito and contracted encephalitis. She was in a coma in an Army hospital in an iron lung, and my parents were admonished to make haste to see her while she was alive.

My mother remembers bending over Nadyne in the hospital and saying, "Nadyne, it's Mom. Mom's here," and looking for any sign that she might have been able to hear, understand, and take comfort. Instead, Nadyne continued to lay motionless and soon after went home to be with our Lord. A young missionary, Jim Elliot, once said shortly before dying on the mission field, "He is no fool who gives what he cannot keep to gain what he cannot lose." Nadyne was indeed no fool.

Right after Nadyne's funeral in Japan, my parents returned to the States, where they watched their other daughter, me, about seven months' pregnant with their grandchild, pack my belongings to launch on to the mission fields, first in Puerto Rico and then onto the island of St. Croix, which we knew little about back then. There probably aren't the words to describe the battle going on inside Mom's heart, having just returned from having one daughter die on the mission field, to see her youngest daughter, who is expecting a baby, packing to leave her and go onto the mission field as well.

Surely, there was a part of her that wanted to grab onto me and never let me go, but instead, she chose to trust the Lord with my life and her yet-unborn grandchild's life as she graciously helped me to pack. She reminded herself that she had asked the Lord to cause both of her daughters to serve Him, and indeed both had made that choice. She did the best thing she could do: She trusted God completely, even with what was most precious and irreplaceable, and even when her own heart must have been slayed with a million sorrows.

Clif and I grieved over losing Nadyne too, but at the same time, life was marching forward. We said goodbye to our parents and boarded a plane for the unknown. We didn't have all the answers for why things happened the way they did or how things might unfold in the future; we just served and trusted a God Who did.

Vieques: Yet More Prep

Thou therefore endure hardness as a
good soldier of Jesus Christ.

—Timothy 2:3

On the first day of August 1956, we boarded a plane to Puerto Rico. Don met us there and said he had already begun to build the Christian radio station on Vieques Island. He needed some hands to help dig trenches for underground radio cables. I was to stay in Puerto Rico while Clif went to Vieques to do manual labor. As I was young and in my third trimester of pregnancy, I found that it was very tough to be away from Clif's reassuring presence.

On Vieques, Clif set his hands (with pick and shovel) to digging wet trenches in hazardous, mucky swamp, which was full of deadly malaria virus. Clif also helped to move a huge radio transmitter onto a barge in Puerto Rico and rode with it to Vieques. This was crucial to getting WIVV radio station on the air.

Vieques was a boot camp that helped to prepare us for what we were yet to accomplish. Clif's pick and shovel experience under the hot, tropical sun was a good warmup for building churches on St. Croix. On St. Croix, Clif continued to use both pick and shovel as he dug and prepared foundation and footings for the three Baptist churches we built there.

Vieques was for a season, and it was a good teacher in many ways. It's good to know when to start something and when to end something or stay on course. We would have never made it to St. Croix if we weren't able to stay on course and stand against the devil's schemes that were designed to prevent us from even setting foot on St. Croix, much less share the good news of the gospel of Jesus Christ there.

Don't kid yourself: When God calls you to do a work for Him, there will be opposition, fear, impossibilities, and unknowns. The trip to your destination may be turbulent, but determine to stay on course. We're glad we did, but here's what we learned as we were meeting the challenges of staying on course.

Stay on Course

Notwithstanding the Lord stood with me and strengthened me, that by me the preaching might be fully known, and that all the Gentiles might hear.

—Timothy 4:17

Whenever God plants a seed in our heart that He wants to grow, like the vision He gave us for St. Croix, the enemy comes along and tries to devour that precious seed before it can even take root, much less come to fruition. You must not only know what God's will is for your life, but you must guard it and stay on course. We are not to be ignorant of Satan's devices.

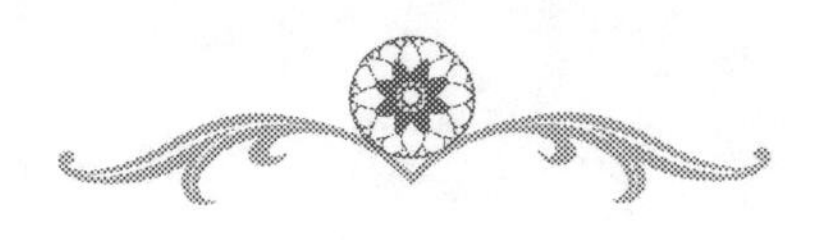

Touchdown

On October 1, 1956, Don Luttrell flew us from Vieques, Puerto Rico, to St. Croix in his little airplane. We were loaded with two suitcases, boxes, a trunk, and a folded baby-pen given to us in Vieques; my lap was full (baby on board). It felt a bit scary and uncertain, taking off in a little one-engine airplane on a short dirt runway, trying to gain air speed and altitude as we skimmed the treetops along the beach. We were looking forward to finally being where our hearts already were, our island St. Croix.

Everyone knows that it is fun to dream big dreams. To walk them is something different. On the day we arrived, we were dropped off in the rain at the airport with our few belongings in tow and not knowing a soul. Indeed, no one was even expecting us but God. We had all the time in the world to watch as Don's little airplane grew smaller and smaller and finally disappeared into the distant sky as it headed back to Vieques. It was a good thing God was already waiting on us. Our Good Shepherd guided us forward in terrain that He knew well. God is with you wherever you go, always.

Landing in St. Croix was like landing in a different world, and in fact, it was a different world for us. The people were different in race, customs, and background, and although they spoke English, it was with a Crucian dialect, and we had to make an effort to tune our ears to it in order to understand what they were saying. And we were very different to them too.

Upon our arrival, I was nine months' pregnant, and we had two hundred dollars. A hotel would have cost a good share of that, and the only other alternative was an unfurnished house that Don had secured for us. We went to a store and bargained for a single rollaway cot. The store owner glanced at my stomach and gave us a good price with installment payments. When he learned that we didn't even own a vehicle to haul it away, he said, "Here, take my truck," and handed us the keys. God is so gracious.

We set up our luxurious single rollaway cot in our empty house. Soon after, Clif converted a shipping crate into a functional piece of furniture to sit on, complete with a cushion. This helped me to stay a little more comfortable as our son Mark tumbled and kicked happily inside my belly.

We also managed to locate a good deal on an old canvas-top Jeep from a car dealer in Frederiksted. Its price of $600 included random holes in the floorboards that provided natural air conditioning, along with its open sides. We were blessed with good terms: twenty-five dollars down and twenty-five dollars a month. We were now rolling. Don't be discouraged when you start small; that's how most things start. Be thankful for what you have, and God will add to you what you need when you need it.

It was October 25, 1956, just twenty-four days after our arrival on St. Croix, when Clif and I boarded our trusty

Jeep in the darkness of the night and pointed it towards the clinic at Frederiksted. Remember, earlier on I told you to make sure to pack a sense of humor to take along on the mission field? Well, Clif and I laughed along the way as I lifted my feet on occasion to avoid the rain splashing up through the floorboard of our Jeep. But as my pains became more intense, Clif slowed down to an abrupt stop several times in an effort to miss huge potholes in the road. I remember that at one place in the road, someone had stuck a tree limb in one of the potholes so that cars and donkey carts would be aware of the huge hole.

We finally arrived at the Frederiksted clinic, and soon after, our precious son Mark was delivered by a Crucian female doctor. Baby Bubar weighed 7 pounds and 6 ounces, and he was a bundle of joy. As a Crucian-born child, he was added to the seventeen thousand population of St. Croix and deposited into a little, no-frills basket for Jeep transport. What a precious gift from God. And he still is, although he's a bit bigger now, a man of fifty-nine, and has outgrown his basket.

One day, I turned the radio on, and what a surprise it was to hear WIVV, the Christian radio station broadcasting from Vieques. It was only a few weeks ago that Clif and Dave Crane had dug trenches and carried a huge transmitter on a barge. Now, we were hearing Christian music and well-known Bible preachers and teachers and the "Don and Dave Show." Everyone loved the Christian music request program Don and Dave aired every afternoon. Christian programs could be heard throughout the Caribbean. How refreshing.

Sadly to say, both Don and Dave have slipped away to their heavenly home, also Ruth Luttrell, Don's wife, has joined them. I remember Ruth flew over from Vieques to visit me in the clinic when Mark was born.

She said, "Oh, LeEllen, your baby is so cute." Those words, coming from someone I knew, and being in a clinic where I knew no one, made my day. God is so good.

St. Croix touchdown

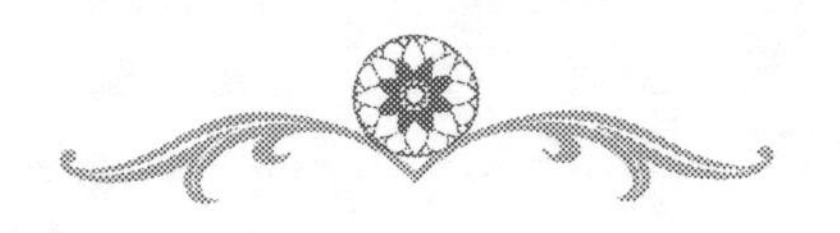

Bubba Git Mash Up

He shall not be afraid of evil tidings:
his heart is fixed, in the Lord.
—Psalm 112:7

Every morning in April 1959, the sun beat down from the cloudless blue sky. One day, there was a big event going on in St. Croix; it was Horse Racing Day at the racetrack across from the Alexander Hamilton Airport. Taxi cars, buses, and automobiles were traveling to and from the airport, transporting family, friends, and visitors to see the horse races. Clif had driven to a store and would return home soon.

Suddenly, I heard someone pounding and yelling at our door. Several Crucian children were hollering, "Miss Bubba, Miss Bubba, Pasta Bubba git boot up! He git mash up! Come! Come! We sho' ya whey he be."

Mark was six years old at the time; I took him in my arms and hurriedly followed the boys down to the corner, where there was a crowd of Crucian people gathered near the road. I saw Bibles, hymnals, and tracts scattered all over the road and covered with oil and dirt. I saw a police car and a policeman. I saw our Volkswagen bus turned upside down on the hood of a heavy, full-sized car.

With Mark still in my arms, I squeezed through

the crowd, determined to see my husband still alive. I finally got a glimpse of him surrounded by a crowd of Crucians. They were staring in amazement at Clif, who was standing straight and tall, with his hands on his hips and not even so much as a drop of blood on his white shirt. He was unharmed. Furthermore, the other driver involved in the accident was not hurt, either. Everyone wondered how these two were unharmed when the wreck had been so bad.

The Crucian man who was involved in the accident had been very drunk and speeding at about eighty miles per hour in a twenty-five-mile speed zone as he was coming home from the races.

Clif said, "When the car hit our bus, our bus flew up into the air like a tin can."

Clif was knocked to one side of the bus and then to the other. He slid across the seat so fast that when he hit the door, the weight of his body opened it. While the bus was still in the air, Clif was thrown out and landed on all fours under it. On hands and knees, he quickly crawled out from under the bus just before I arrived. Our little Volkswagen bus was totaled, and the Crucian man received a ticket.

A Crucian nurse who lived nearby witnessed the whole accident, and she ran out expecting to see a dead man. When she saw Clif standing tall and straight with his hands on his hips, she hugged him and said, "Oh, you must be a preacher. Thank God. Only a preacher could live through that."

I thought of this verse: "The angel of the Lord encamps around those who fear him, and He delivers them."

What to make of all this? "And we know that in all

things God works for the good of those who love him, who have been called according to his purpose." God worked this out to be a testimony throughout the island. Everyone heard about the accident and had to wonder at God's miracle.

We believe that God spared Clif's life because our work on St. Croix was in no way finished. We went on in the strength of God to build and pastor three churches, Frederiksted Baptist, Sunny Isle Baptist, and Southgate Baptist. We were able to reach many people for Jesus, including a Spanish couple, Ping and Carmen Navarro, who went onto build a church for Spanish-speaking people. We also were able to help other pastors and missionaries on St. Croix and other islands.

The devil didn't limit his efforts to attempting to "mash up Pastor Bubba." He also attempted to mash up our son in a different way. You see, when you go on missions, you go planning to shape the lives of others. But others shape your lives, as well. Mash-up efforts know no age limit … but God can have the final say.

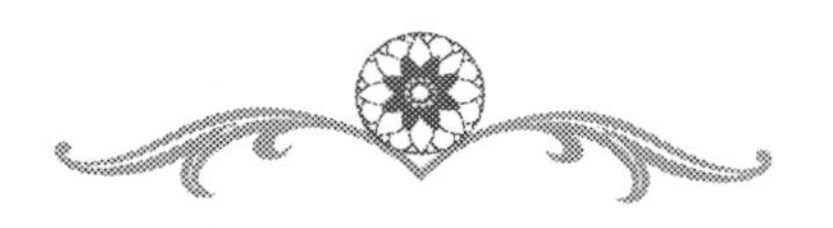

Kindergarten Lessons

Every experience God gives us, every person
He puts in our lives, is the perfect preparation
for the future that only He can see.
—Corrie Ten Boom

The kindergarten class that our son Mark attended met in a building near a government housing project in Frederiksted. The class was filled to capacity with about sixteen little Crucian children, including Mark. Even though he was born on St. Croix, and therefore a Crucian, his blond hair, fair skin, and blue eyes made the other five-year-olds think that he was a foreigner and invited unwanted attention.

One day, Mark came home from his class, crying and upset. He said, "Some of the children were peeping their heads under the bathroom stall when I was in the bathroom. They giggled and laughed at me and called me 'whitey-pa-hey.' I don't want to ever go back to that school again."

It must have been a traumatic experience for a little five-year-old.

Another day, as a Crucian boy was walking by our house, he hollered at Mark, "Go bac hom, wher' yo cum frum, whitey-pa-hey!"

I heard Mark reply deliberately in a Crucian dialet, "Dis iss' ma hom! I bon he'ya."

"Island born" and a Crucian accent made a difference. The Crucian boy never bothered Mark again.

However, others did, and for as long as Mark lived on the island, he looked different from the other kids, no matter where he went. This shaped his life. He had to learn to stand his ground, communicate in a strategically relevant way, and at other times simply run fast.

God didn't make a mistake when he chose to grow Mark on an island. God has taken what was meant for Mark's harm and turned it for his good. Today, our son has a strong and gritty personality; he is a man who will not hesitate to stand his ground and say what he means in a way that is clearly understood. A lot of men are too afraid to do that. Our son isn't. In today's climate, we need good men who aren't afraid to stand their ground and who know how to. We pray that at every turn, Mark will be a man who dares to say yes to God and who will walk in obedience to God.

Did you know that God can take everything that shaped your life and turn it for your good? With God, even your messes can become your message. Put your life in the Master's hands. And God will create a masterpiece for His glory, as only He can do. Did you know that there's a particular group of people who have a very hard time ever saying yes to God? I'll tell you who they are, and why that is.

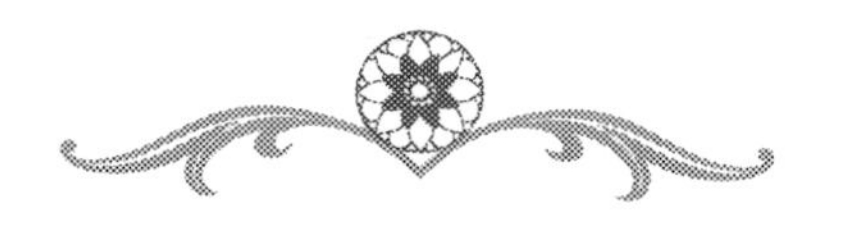

Searching Everywhere

And the Lord said unto the servant. Go out into
the highways and hedges and compel them
to come in, that my house maybe filled.

—Luke 14:23

You know how some people spend their time looking for garage sales, bargains, or treasures? Well, Clif and I still have a daily habit of looking everywhere for lost souls. We just knew that every day, we would find them in a multitude of places and that more than anything, they needed to hear the gospel of Jesus Christ. That explains why we spent our time going house to house, visiting people we had never met and teaching Bible lessons, why we would go to the hospitals, the lepers' colony, and the boys' home. We had open-air outreaches where Clif played the trumpet and I played the accordion in efforts to attract crowds. We befriended children in the streets, held Bible clubs for them, and hosted Carib Camp for youth during the summers. We didn't have to have a church building to get started. After all, first things first: God's heart is for *people.* And then a church building is needed for the people.

As we worked to meet the needs of the people, God also saw to meeting our needs for a church. It would be the first Baptist church on the island of St. Croix. God says, "Who despises the day of small things?" We started in small ways and even started out preaching in ruins, but God added His blessing to our efforts. Be found faithful in the small things, and then God will trust you with more.

You may be thinking, *Well, doing all that stuff is fine for you missionaries, but I've really messed up my life and don't see how I could do much for God now. I've made too many mistakes and have too many regrets. I had my chance and blew it. I guess I have to sit on the sidelines and give offerings so others can do good works.*

If that's you, then you've got God's interest. He's in the restoration business. In Psalms, David said, "He restoreth my soul." David should surely know. He committed adultery with another man's wife and then had her husband killed. Talk about making a mess of things. Yet he said that God restores his soul. That's what God wants to do for your life. Your sin is not so bad that Jesus's blood can't cleanse it. God looks beyond faults and failures and sees your value; after all, He made you. He paid a tremendous price on the cross to see you saved and fully restored.

It's not over until it's over, so leave the devil's lies and the past behind, and make a choice today to walk forward with a God Who restores. Don't limit your future by what you did in the past. It's time to take the lid off your life, forgive yourself, forget the past, and press forward to all that God still has for you today. It's no accident that you're reading this book. God has a plan for your life, and it's still on. Press forward. Dare to say yes to a future with God that doesn't have to look anything like the past. God uses all kinds of people with all kinds of pasts and personalities.

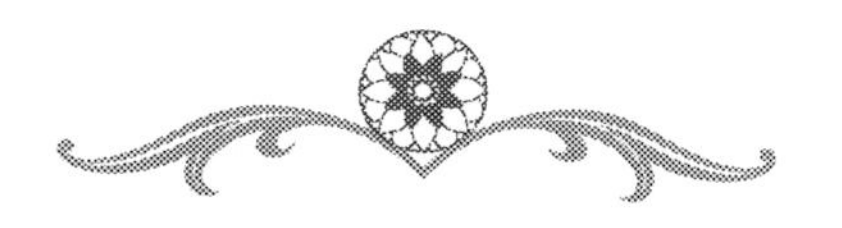

The Same Dilemma Today

Why sit here until we die?

—2 Kings 7:3

In 1956, God sent us to visit the leper colony at Richmond Estate in Christiansted. Leprosy was still a terribly contagious disease back then, so the lepers were quarantined. They couldn't leave the colony to attend church, so God brought us to them. Leprosy was a creeping disease that destroys the body. It begins with a tingling in the hand, nose, or ears, and then it becomes numbness in the hands and feet. A leper can stub their toe or hurt their finger and not even feel it. Some of the lepers were missing parts of their bodies; toes were missing, and some had small, stubby fingers. Some of their faces were horribly disfigured, or they were missing an ear. They had lost the sense of pain and were coated with white splotches all over their bodies.

The director of the colony was all for us having church services and Bible studies for the lepers, so we held a service every Friday afternoon. The lepers were so happy to have visitors, because not many people came to visit them. Even if a spouse or child came to visit, they couldn't hug, touch, or kiss them. They loved seeing our little baby, Mark. Some of them would come near our open Jeep where Mark was lying in a basket on the back seat. They knew they weren't to touch us or come too close. Sometimes, their curious fingers wanted to reach into the Jeep to touch his blond hair.

I would have to tell them, "No, no. You mustn't touch baby Mark."

They longed to have someone touch them.

The lepers had many sad stories to tell us. One young man in his early twenties said he and his high school sweetheart planned to be married. After graduation, he applied for a marriage license and had a blood test. The blood test returned positive for leprosy. The wedding was called off, and their hearts were utterly broken. This man attended the Bible studies every Friday afternoon. He heard Clif preach the gospel of salvation for the first time in his life. We gave him a Bible, and as he studied it and his lessons, he learned that Jesus loved him and died for his sins. One day, he asked Jesus to forgive his sins and to save him and to become his Savior. He realized that God still had a plan for his life.

After a number of years passed, an announcement was made to the lepers on St. Croix that their disease was in remission and was no longer considered contagious. Leprosy had been eradicated with preventative medicine, and the leper colony disbanded. Lepers were set free to live wherever they chose to live. Some stayed on St. Croix, living and dwelling among us. Others went to neighboring islands in the Caribbean. The lepers who received Jesus rejoiced that they were set free from their sins when they put their faith and trust in Jesus and now were set free from the leper colony. They were freed twice.

The Bible tells us that lepers were outcasts because the disease was contagious. Leprosy was spread by contact with one another. In Bible times, lepers were rejected and sent off to a secluded area; they lived without hope. No one wanted to be near them, not their spouse, their children, or their friends. When anyone came around, the leper was obligated to call out, "Unclean! Unclean!" No one wanted to get near them or touch them. How would you feel if you could never be hugged or kissed and you had to tell everyone you came in contact with to stay away?

There are people who are living like lepers today. There are things that have happened to them, challenges that they have, setbacks, fears, debt, secret sins, addictions, hatred, bitterness, lies that were told them, and a host of other conditions that keep them from experiencing the full life that God has for them and from being fully embraced by society. They feel like their lives are rotting away, little by little, but unlike the lepers, they *can* feel the pain. It's a miserable way to live. And Jesus is willing to set them free.

Perhaps as you read this, you or someone you know can identify with being held back by some situation in their lives. I want to tell you another leper story: In the Bible, there were four lepers, and they were dying, not only because of their leprosy but also because there was a severe famine in the city, which was under siege by an enemy.

The lepers were a sensible bunch; they had no time for wishful thinking or pity parties. The way they reasoned turned their lives around, and the same type of reasoning could help to turn yours around too:

"They said to another, 'Why sit here until we die? If we say, we will enter into the city, we will die there. And if we sit still here, we will die also.'

So let's go over to the camp of the Arameans and surrender. If they spare us, we live; if they kill us, then we die" (2 Kings 7:3–4).

They knew their lives weren't working. They knew doing the same things the same way would only keep leading them on the same downward spiral. They determined to do something different, and their lives took an awesome turn for the better. They discovered an abundance of what they needed and blessings besides. They were glad they moved past their fears and moved towards a better future.

With the way the economy is, with the way the world is going, with the situations you may be facing, you may have come to the same conclusion: "Why sit here until I die?" You might be saying to yourself, "Hey, my life is not working. If I keep on going this way, I'll have more of the same. I'm going nowhere fast, except getting older and deeper in this ditch. I am willing to risk. I am willing to do something different. I feel desperate and under siege as the lepers. I have to do something different."

Now is the time to give your life fully to Jesus and say yes to His will. Why would you want to keep a life that is not working? Give God the life that you have, and He will give you the one He has for you. You get the better deal. Dare to say yes to God. He'll make the difference you've been looking for, wanting, and needing. Trust Him. Take a moment to commit your life fully to Him now so you can turn the page and start a new chapter. God is waiting on you to talk to Him right now.

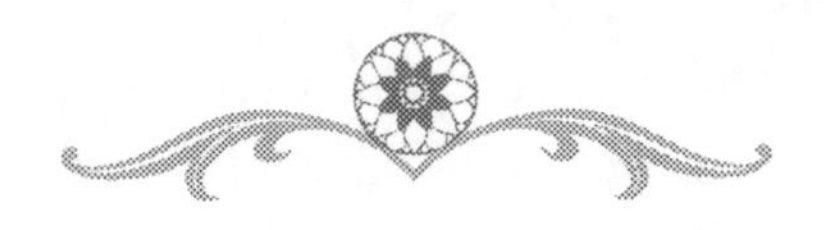

Fishermen Go Where the Fish Are

And Jesus said unto them, come ye after me, and
I will make you to become fishers of men.
—Mark 1:17

There are lots of fish tales floating about St. Croix, but here's one I want to share with you. It began one hot afternoon at the fish market by the sea in Frederiksted.

Clif was buying fish when he overheard a couple of men telling fish tales. One of the men was a policeman. He said, "Pastor Bubar, come with us sometime and you can see how we harpoon huge sharks. It's a good sport."

Jesus hung out with fishermen, and Clif thought it sounded like a good idea too. He knew the policeman through sharing Christ with him and inviting him to our church in Frederiksted.

The day came that Clif climbed into their small twelve-foot rowboat, and he and the two fishermen rowed to an area where they had previously anchored a donkey carcass to attract sharks. The wind blew, and the waves splashed against the little boat, tossing it up and down in the Caribbean Sea. As the men rowed up close to the donkey carcass, sharks were swimming around it and biting chunks from it in a massive feeding frenzy.

Suddenly, one of the fishermen threw his harpoon, and it was a straight shot. It lodged into a huge shark, nearly the size of the boat. The shark took off with the harpoon in him, and the water turned blood red as the boat trailed behind him. A struggle with the shark ensued as the men toiled with the long rope connected to the harpoon. The shark would dive deep and then come up, sometimes coming so near to the boat that the policeman would hit the shark on the head with his knife. Clif was concerned that the shark might strike the boat in such a way that it would sink it. He decided that this was a good time to inject a little logic into the situation in order to avoid such a dilemma, so he asked the policeman why he didn't just shoot the shark with his pistol.

The question proved to be terribly amusing for the policemen, who, in between fits of laughter, managed to reply, "That's no sport."

Clif's face had probably turned a beautiful oceanic shade of blue by the time a motor boat came to tow them safely back to shore. Perhaps there was nothing to be alarmed at after all, he reasoned quietly to himself, as these were two Crucian fishermen that obviously considered shark hunting a mere sport. What's the old saying, "All's well that ends well"? Still, this was Clif's first shark adventure, and dry land never looked better.

When the fishermen arrived back on shore with the shark, Clif felt enough in the clear to breathe a huge sigh of relief. But just when he thought it was safe, the fishermen realized that they had lost the harpoon pole, which had sunk to the bottom. They announced that they (fishermen and Clif) would leave the huge shark on the sandy beach and row back out to the donkey carcass, where sharks were still actively feeding and the water still ran blood red. One of the fishermen, determined to retrieve the harpoon, dove down amid the sharks and surfaced with the harpoon pole and climbed matter-of-factly back into the boat as if he had just stopped off at a store to pick up a loaf of bread. No wonder Jesus chose a bunch of fishermen; fishing is not for sissies. Those fishermen really went after the fish and took a risk in order to retrieve what was lost. When fishing for souls, you've got to leave the safe shoreline of the church and go to where the fish are; sometimes, that feels about as warm and fuzzy as a shark fishing trip.

Once ashore, the fishermen enjoyed some fame from their large catch, and more people came to watch the fishermen butcher the shark as news of it spread. Lots of Crucian talk and excitement was in the air as the fishermen prepared the shark that was almost the length of the boat.

Now, here's what fishermen know about sharks:

Sharks give birth to their living young, and this particular shark was full of one-foot baby sharks. The tiger shark is one of the most prolific breeders, being known to give birth to fifty-seven offspring in one batch. The newborn sharks must fend for themselves, and it is not uncommon for them to be consumed by their own mother.

No other fish can match a shark in jaw power. The bite of a shark is measured in tons, not pounds. Sharks help keep the ocean clean by feeding on the carcasses of small or large animals, no matter how rotten they might be; all is devoured quickly by these hungry predators.

Every conceivable object found in the sea can at some time or other be recovered from the stomachs of sharks. The remains of turtles, stingrays, octopus, sea urchin, starfish, pieces of coral, shellfish, clams, and other marine animals and plants have been found in sharks. The most unexpected things found in sharks include cans and bottles, pieces of wood, cork, plastic rope, metal, wire, rocks, paper, and cardboard. I remember an announcement that we heard on the radio in the Caribbean that reported a man's arm was found, with the wristwatch still running, inside the belly of a shark.

A shark can eat in any position and often gulps down food rather than using its teeth to chew it. Usually, sharks carefully survey the object to be eaten, gradually moving closer and circling their food. Finally, the shark moves confidently in for a rapid catch.

Like fishermen, try to always know a little about the fish (souls) that you are fishing for. Fishermen also use the right bait for the right fish; should you really use those hymnals when reaching out to a bunch of burly bikers up to their eyeballs in Budweisers? Give it some thought. We are fishermen, and we're to catch souls for Jesus, so let's launch out into the deep where the fish are and get busy. Here are a few of our fishing tales as we fished for souls; let's begin with the Turtle Guy, who was fairly inebriated, so more love than words were needed:

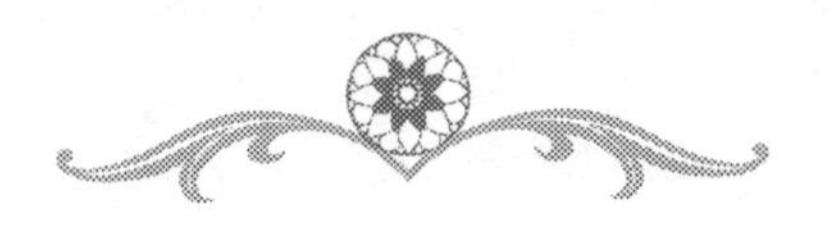

Turtle Guy Does a Turnaround

Love never fails.
—1 Corinthians 13:8

I still have a very nice turtle shell in my home that oddly enough was given to me by a man who had just finished cursing at me. Clif and I were flying home on furlough to the States when stormy weather made it necessary to overnight on Caicos Island. Clif was checking us into a hotel, and I sat nearby to wait. Suddenly, a native man came over to me and started cursing me.

He said, "You *@$%#% white woman!"

I replied, "Jesus loves you."

He said it again, and I repeated, "Jesus loves you."

He asked, "Who are you?"

I replied, "I'm a missionary."

The man was so horrified at what he had done that he came and knelt down in front of me and said, "Please forgive me."

I could tell by this time that the man was drunk on rum. He excused himself and said he would be back. He went into a gift shop and returned to present me with a beautiful lacquered turtle shell that measured about a foot by fourteen inches, to underscore his apology for mistreating me and using bad language. He explained that he hunted turtles and prepared them to sell at the gift shop. I accepted his apology and the lovely turtle shell and gave him a tract with scriptures telling him how to be saved.

I asked him to please read it when he was sober and then told him again, "Jesus loves you."

I often wonder what might have happened if I had not turned the other cheek but responded in offense. As it was, the Holy Spirit spoke to the man's heart when I replied in the name of Jesus. How powerful is that Name above all names.

I believe that the Turtle Guy still remembered the love of Jesus when he sobered up enough to read the tract that I gave him and reach out thirstily for the living waters that are found only in Jesus. When you don't know what to give a person whose behavior is difficult, give them the love of Jesus. There is no defense against love. Sometimes, even church people need an extra dose of love.

You can never share the love of Jesus with the wrong person. God rewards us in different ways.

You can never share the love of Jesus with the wrong person. God rewards us in different ways.

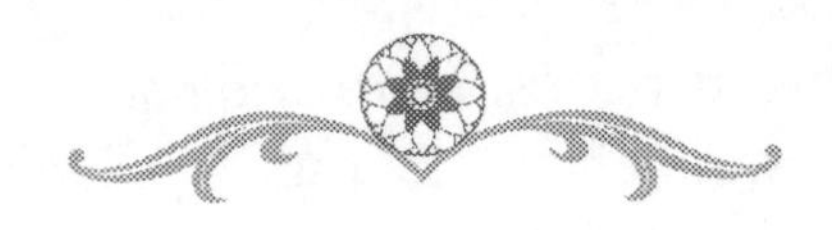

Poison in the Cup and in the Soul

He that saith he is in the light and hateth his brother is in darkness even until now.
—1 John 2:9

It was about midnight, and the New Year was being ushered in with horns blaring, firecrackers, and sirens. We were driving home from the church service when we heard the news headline on the radio: "Four people sink in dinghy in Christiansted Harbor."

The minute we heard the news, we drove to the Christiansted Harbor. We saw three survivors, who had made it to the wharf by swimming. They were dripping wet and shivering from the windy sea breeze. I took my sweater off and wrapped it around one of the ladies who was shivering.

In sobs she said, "My husband has drowned. The last thing he said was, 'Help, I'm drowning!' I turned to help him, and he was gone. Those were the last words out of his mouth. We hollered 'Help' to some boys that were standing on the wharf, but they hollered back, 'Drown, white trash!'"

Her husband had been drunk on liquor, and the people who refused to help were drunk on the poison of hatred. The incident left a woman a widow and her children without a father. Alcoholism and racism never get their fill. Both are destructive forces, and both are present in the church. Of alcohol, an old Japanese proverb states, "First the man takes a drink, then the drink takes a drink, then the drink takes the man." And Proverbs 23:29–32 puts it this way:

"Who has woe? Who has sorrow? Who has strife? Who has complaints? Who has needless bruises? Who has bloodshot eyes?

"They that tarry long at the wine; they that go to seek mixed wine.

"Look that tarry long at the wine; when it is red, when it giveth his color in the cup when it moveth itself aright.

"At the last it biteth like a serpent, and stingeth like an adder."

Racism also bites like a snake and poisons like a viper. The woman widowed that New Year's Eve will remember its bite for the rest of her life. If racism was only found amid revelers down at the dock, that might not be as surprising as it is when a church group imports it from the States. A church group from the United States came to minister in our church in St. Croix and brought with them racist attitudes that were still quite commonly found where they were from. The love of the people in our church towards these visitors, regardless of their racist attitudes, was the catalyst to revival and served to break down the dividing walls that were separating us from all truly dwelling in the unity of Christ, Revival broke out because our congregation ministered the love and forgiveness of Christ to the visiting church group in a way that forever touched their hearts and changed their attitudes towards brothers and sisters of different races.

Psalm 133:1 declares, "Behold, how good and how pleasant it is for brethren to dwell together in unity." When our guests left the island, they left behind their racism on the altar and brought back changed hearts and attitudes with them to the States. What if our church members had chosen to take offense and not turn the other cheek? Fortunately, they went God's way. They knew that "love suffers long and is kind" (1 Corinthians 13:4). And that love conquers all.

One thing is for sure when you dare to say yes to God: Offenses will surely come, and you will be tested.

A young pastor once asked a very seasoned older pastor who had a very successful ministry, "If you could only give me one piece of advice, what would it be?"

The older pastor answered without hesitation, "If you don't get bitter, you'll make it."

The love of Christ can conquer the bitter poisons of hatred and prejudice and fill a person's heart so they thirst no more.

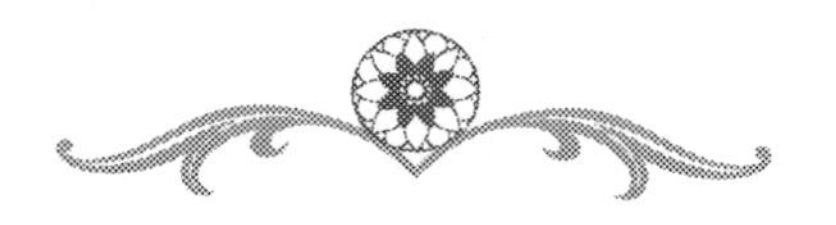

Margie's Beauty Salon

When you want to tell the world, tell a hairdresser.
—Anonymous

Everyone in town knew Margie and needed Margie; after all, she was the hairdresser on Main Street in Christiansted. Margie had golden hair and a heart of gold to match. She took in stray animals, the poor, homeless people, and derelicts. Her reputation was such that they all knew she would give them food and money. Margie believed God when He said, "Do unto others as you would have them do unto you." Further, she thought by obeying this command, it would help her merit a place in heaven someday.

One day, while Margie was doing my hair, she spoke of the many people she had helped. I realized she genuinely enjoyed helping people and that she genuinely wanted to be sure of going to heaven someday too. Margie had diligently read the Bible almost all the way through.

Margie, who gave so much love, hadn't found it yet in her own life. She had been married four times and was getting ready to get married again for the fifth time at the age of fifty-eight to a man she described as her "dream lover." In the Bible, Jesus had a heart for the woman at the well, and He still has a heart for many like her who are searching for love in relationship after relationship. Jesus led me to minister to Margie what she really needed in her life, and like the woman at the well, Margie would soon run and tell the whole village.

As we chatted, Margie told me that she had adopted seven children and also had several grandchildren. She mentioned that one of the grandchildren had fallen out of a tree and had broken his arm. She remarked with gravity that if he had died, he would have gone to Limbo because he had not been baptized when he was a baby.

I said, "Margie, in reading the Bible, have you read anywhere that babies must be baptized?" Margie shook her head no. I continued, "Would you like to see what the Bible says about baptism?"

She replied, "Oh, yes!" So we set up a time for me to come to her house and see what the Bible had to say about baptism.

When I arrived at Margie's home, I noticed a crucifix, lighted candles, and a large white Bible on a shelf near the front door.

I exclaimed, "You have a beautiful Bible; could we use it to study from?"

She agreed and remarked that it was a Catholic Bible.

I said, "Your Bible is similar to mine. Some words are different. We can compare Bibles and see where they differ, but first let's see what the Bible says about baptism."

I knew she was very concerned about her grandson not being baptized as an infant. She took the huge white Bible to a table where we studied on the topic of baptism. She underlined each of the verses in her Catholic Bible comparing them with the same verses in my Schofield Bible. She saw that both Bibles had the same meaning but were worded a little differently. I had her pattern each of the verses through her Bible like a chain reference, so she could know where to find the verses.

When we finished the study on baptism, she exclaimed, "Oh, Mrs. Bubar, I didn't know the Bible was so plain to understand. I've learned more tonight than I have learned all of my life in the Catholic church."

Now that she had the knowledge and understanding of the meaning of baptism, she was not as concerned with the baptism of her grandson. He first needed to be saved. So we studied the topic, "How to be saved." As we read verse by verse in the Bible, she saw that "saved" is a Bible term, not just a term that the Baptist uses. She underlined the verses, marking them in her Bible, putting topics and key verses in the back of the book.

When we finished that Bible study, I asked, "Margie, wouldn't you like to ask Jesus to save you now, tonight? Wouldn't you like to know where you're going to spend eternity?"

She exclaimed, "Oh, yes! This is what I have been looking for all of my life." That night, Margie prayed, confessing she was a sinner, and asked Jesus to save her.

It was the beginning of a new life for Margie; she began telling everyone that she was saved and that she had become a Christian. As a hairdresser, she talked to a lot of people and had a captive audience. People saw the change in Margie's life. Her language changed, she quit smoking, even her beauty salon changed with Christian literature, tracts, and Bibles taking over the prime spot where she used to display wigs for sale.

Margie didn't marry for the fifth time. She found what she had always been looking for: the lover of her soul,

Jesus Christ, her Savior. She found happiness and joy in serving the Lord in her beauty salon. She even shared her testimony with the priest in the Catholic church she had attended for most of her life. Margie shared Jesus not only with everyone who came into her beauty salon, but also with those on the street outside of her salon. God was in control of Margie's life.

Isn't it amazing when we know the Lord and are willing to share Him with others? God opens doors in the right places at the right times.

Margie attended the Frederiksted Baptist Church, where we ministered. She was baptized and became a member of the church and a worker for Jesus. I thank God that I responded to God's leading when He opened the door for me to share with Margie in her beauty salon and to follow up with her with a Bible study in her home. There are many opportunities to share Jesus, if we dare to say yes to God.

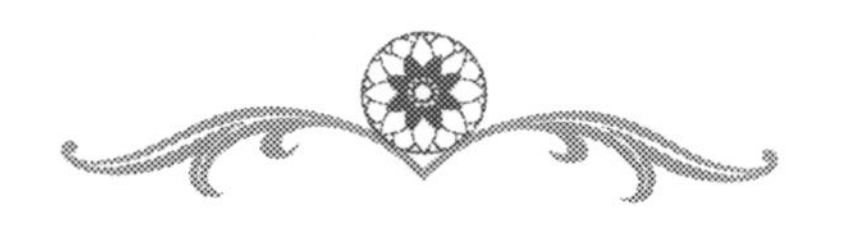

A Special Visit

Believe on the Lord Jesus Christ and
thou shalt be saved and thy house.

—Acts 16:31

One day, Clif and I were driving on a dusty, bumpy dirt road on St. Croix in the Karavel area. We noticed a bright pink house with a red metal roof on a little hilltop. There was an elderly couple sitting on the porch. We drove up the driveway and stepped up to their porch to meet them. They welcomed us with kind and smiling faces. The man's sense of humor broke the ice, and he made us feel at home. They mentioned they were of Danish and Crucian descent.

We shared our faith in Jesus with the couple and told of our endeavor to reach people for Jesus and plant churches on St. Croix. Both of them were very empathetic toward us and toward our interest in the people of St. Croix. The man said that Jehovah Witnesses had often come to his home, and he felt that they were good people serving God too. They studied the Bible with him and his wife and their four children. He said that the Jehovah Witnesses were using one of his buildings in Christiansted for a Kingdom Hall.

After a pleasant visit, they urged us to come back

and visit them again. We had made the acquaintance of some really down-to-earth and honest people who were searching for God and in need of a Savior. We felt God's touch on the contact made that day, so we returned to visit them with a purpose in mind. We shared with them that Jesus became God in the flesh and that He shed His blood for sinners and that He became our Savior. We testified that we had put our trust in Him and that we have eternal life.

We knew that it was hard for them to accept that Jesus is God because Jehovah Witnesses had taught them that Jesus is just a God, not the one true God. We didn't argue but kept the door open by praying for them and keeping in touch.

Sometimes, when we saw them sitting on the porch, we would stop by. The man was interesting to talk to, and he liked to sit and chat. He talked about his farm, and as we looked out from his porch, we could see his sheep grazing in the field and the chicken coops. When Mark was a little boy, this man gave him a dozen white leghorn chickens.

The chickens came into good use when we had our first Christian Youth Camp at Davis Beach. We enclosed a little kitchen with cardboard under the trees. We had saved up enough of the eggs from the chickens to feed about twenty children breakfast. We put the eggs in Tupperware containers in our makeshift kitchen, but that night, the kitchen had a visitor who was able to open the container and raid all of the eggs, leaving nothing but eggshells on the ground in the morning. The culprit was a mongoose (a small Indian animal) that is known for killing snakes and keeping St. Croix snake-free. The mongoose had stolen the eggs and carried each one up a tree in its mouth, sucking out the inside of the eggs and dropping the shells on the ground underneath.

Anyway, back to the family that gave us the chickens: Their daughter-in-law was a born-again Christian and was looking for a church home. She happened to meet Clif at the gas station her husband owned in Frederiksted and inquired about church service times. She visited our church and then began studying the Bible with me. She expressed her desire to follow the Lord, so Clif baptized her at the Frederiksted Baptist Church. Her mother came all the way from Puerto Rico to witness her daughter's baptism. In the following weeks, her daughter's life proved to be a testimony to God's wonderful saving grace.

Clif began studying the Bible with her husband, the elderly couple's son. He accepted Jesus as Lord and Savior and also decided to quit smoking for good. His father couldn't believe that his son had quit smoking for good and agreed that he would go to church with his son if he could stay off cigarettes for a certain length of time. Well, the son kept his end of the bargain, but the father didn't come to church. Instead, he requested that Clif meet with the Jehovah Witness pastor to discuss the Bible. (The man was the director of all the Jehovah Witnesses in the Caribbean.) He said that he could never get a Protestant pastor to meet with his Jehovah Witness pastor.

A date was set for the meeting, and six of us met at the son's home. Present were the Jehovah Witness pastor, the elderly father, the son and his wife, and Clif and I. The Jehovah Witness pastor came with books as large as the old Sears & Roebuck catalogs. Clif brought the Bible and a Jehovah Witness Green Bible. The discussion went on for about four hours, and it became clear to all present that the Jehovah Witness pastor not only did not believe the Protestant Bible, but also did not even believe his own translation of the Bible, nor had he ever come to the saving grace of Jesus Christ.

Soon afterward, the father accepted Jesus Christ as his Savior. Later, his wife and most of their sons and their families became born-again Christians and members of Baptist churches.

We are so thankful that we dared to say yes to the Lord's leading to stop at the little pink house on the hillside. God used a home visit that helped begin a ministry that saw almost a whole family come to Him as Savior. Praise to our wonderful Lord and Savior, Jesus Christ.

It is important to know the scriptures to present them clearly to people who are confused about what truth is and what is not. It is also important to live a life of integrity, as this is also a powerful witness in and of itself; there will be no opportunity for people to be confused by any variation between what you are telling them and what you are living. I want to tell you about one of the times my integrity was tested and what the results were:

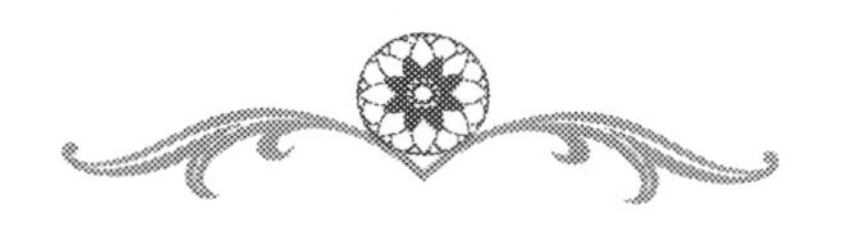

The Power of Integrity

Let your light so shine before men, that they may see your good works and glorify your Father in heaven.
—Matthew 5:16

It was a dark and rainy night. A friend and I went to a concert at the Christiansted High School. I parked the car, and when I opened the door, the handle slipped out of my hand, causing my car door to strike the new car parked next to me. My heart skipped a beat.

My friend advised, "Move the car, and no one will ever know."

I said, "No, I can't do that. I need to leave a note on the car and let them know what happened."

I found a piece of paper and wrote, "As I was getting out of my car, the door slipped out of my hand and hit your car door. If you will get in touch with me, I will pay to have the door fixed. I am so sorry." I wrote my phone number, signed it, and left the note attached to their car door.

Then, with a lump in my throat, we trudged through the rain and dark to the concert. Needless to say, my enjoyment of the concert was overshadowed by a great deal of anxiety over the incident. My anxiety lessened as time passed and no one called.

About twelve months later, I was in a store in Christiansted, looking to buy a typewriter. A tall Danish man, the owner of the store, waited on me. I was pondering the price of a typewriter I liked and wondering how I could pay for it.

The man said to me, "Mrs. Bubar, I got your note."

Surprised, I thought, *What note? Why would I be giving him a note?*

Then he said, "I got your note on my car about a year ago."

Then I remembered leaving the note on the new car in the school parking lot.

I said to him, "I felt terrible about it, but you didn't get in touch with me."

He said, "I know. I told my wife it had to be a minister that would be that honest."

I said, "I'm not a minister, but I am a Christian."

Then he said, "Mrs. Bubar, I trust anyone as honest as you were. Take the typewriter and pay for it when you can."

We were able to pay for the typewriter at a good price and on installments.

Several years passed, when one Saturday afternoon, I was visiting a home near the church while Clif was preparing his service notes. I went to say hello to our older friends, the Johansens, who were members of our church.

Ludvig Johansen said, "Mrs. Bubar, I'm so glad you came. My friend and I have been discussing the Bible, but I want you to talk with him."

The friend turned out to be the tall Danish man who owned the store where I purchased the typewriter and who owned the car I dented. He also held a position of influence within the Anglican church.

I shared my testimony and some Bible verses about being born again. I had him read them so he would see them in the Bible and know that it wasn't just a Baptist belief or a tradition. As he read portions of the Bible, and as we discussed them, tears filled his eyes at times. The Holy Spirit must have been revealing truths that were tugging at his heart. When I asked him if he would like to ask Jesus to be his Savior and be born into the family of God, he said he would like that, but he would first talk with his wife.

Ludvig gave him a book to take with him, entitled *Born Again* by Chuck Colson. He asked him to take the book home and read it. We agreed to meet again the next Saturday to discuss it. The Johansens, Clif, and I all prayed for him throughout the week while he was reading the book.

The next Saturday morning, Clif and I met at the Johansens; our Danish friend arrived early. He had read the book, and it was obvious that God had prepared his heart to accept Jesus as his Lord and Savior. We knelt with him in the Johansens' living room as he prayed, accepting Jesus as his Lord and Savior, repenting of his sins, and asking Jesus to save him. That Saturday morning a born-again experience took place in his life, and the angels in heaven were rejoicing over this newborn baby in his late seventies entering the family of God.

Follow-up Bible studies were a blessing, helping him mark his Bible. He was very interested and listened intently. He needed a new Bible, as his had small print; he really liked my Schofield Bible and wanted one for both he and his wife. He gave us money to buy them when we went back to the States for a missionary conference; he also paid for me to replace my Schofield with a new one that was not so worn.

How I praise the Lord that He guided me to dare to say yes to what was right and be true to my testimony as a born-again Christian when I took responsibility for the dented car door. Through that incident, God provided the means to buy a typewriter and blessed me with the gift of a much-needed new Schofield Bible from our new convert friend.

More importantly, God planted the seed of trust in the heart of Mr. Johansen's friend because I demonstrated that Christianity is real. Thus he trusted my verbal witness that the Bible is the Word of God as well as the Holy Spirit's witness, and he accepted Jesus as Savior.

Proverbs 3:5–6 tells us, "Trust in the LORD with all thine heart; and lean not on thine own understanding; in all thy ways acknowledge him, and he shall direct thy paths."

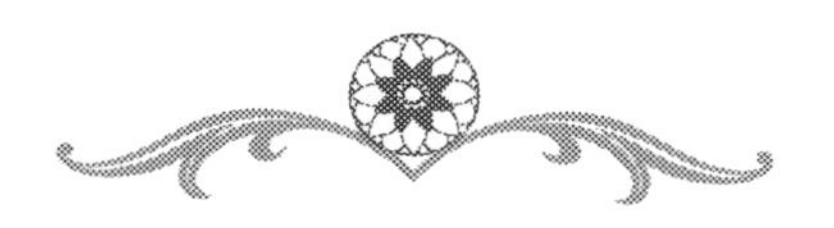

Crucian and Spanish Villages

And he said, Whereunto shall we liken the kingdom of God? Or with what comparison shall we compare it? It is like a grain of mustard seed, which, when it is sown in the earth, is less than all the seeds that be in the earth: But when it is sown, it growth up, and becometh greater than all herbs, and shooteth out of great branches; so that the fowls of the air may lodge under the shadow of it.

One Sunday morning, we were picking up people in our station wagon at Grove Place Village. We stopped at a little house where a mother and her five children lived. They had been faithfully attending services that we held in a rented house in the town of Frederiksted.

A Puerto Rican family lived next door to them. They usually came to their door and watched as the neighbors loaded into our car to go to church. One Sunday, the mother of the five children told us that the Puerto Rican lady next door had asked her if she and her two children could also come to church. We said they were welcome and that we would be glad to have them. We so regretted that we had not invited them before this to our services, but the services were in English, and this little family spoke only Spanish.

On Sunday morning, they were anxiously waiting to go to church. The little girl, Rosa, was in her pretty ruffled dress, and the little boy, Jose, was wearing his dress shirt and tie. Their mother, Carmen, was so happy to be going to church with her children.

After attending several services and hearing the gospel preached, Carmen responded to the invitation given for salvation. She didn't understand English, but the Holy Spirit revealed Bible truth in such a way that she felt her need for Jesus.

I had previously led a lady named Iris to the Lord, and she was bilingual. Iris helped me by interpreting as I led Carmen to Jesus. Later, we learned that Carmen and her husband, Gaspar (known as Ping), were separated. He had a drinking problem; on the weekends, he went to a certain bar in town and drank. Carmen was concerned and told Clif where the bar was and asked him to go there and talk with him.

Now Clif, being a pastor, wasn't in the habit of going into bars; however, this time he felt the Lord was leading him on a mission. Friday night, he went to the bar where Ping hung out and motioned for him to come to the door. They chatted a few minutes, but then Ping went back into the bar, not showing any interest or concern.

We went with Iris to visit Carmen one evening when her husband was there. It was an interesting evening, as Clif read portions of the Bible and explained them. As Iris interpreted, it was as if a dark room suddenly lit up as Ping's eyes were opened to the truth of God's Word and

His saving grace. The Holy Spirit revealed the sinfulness of man and that Jesus died for sinners. As scriptures were read and explained, Ping repented of his sin and asked Jesus to save him and wash his sins away.

Carmen had been saved several months before Ping. She and her two children had been attending the new Frederiksted Baptist Church that Clif was still building. We were having services in it before it was finished. Carmen helped me paint. Clif made the scaffolding to stand on when painting rafters and the high ceiling. While we were painting, Carmen taught me some Spanish, and I taught her some English. We were butchering both languages but understanding enough of it to converse back and forth.

During the week, I showed Carmen how to use flannel-graph pictures to tell Bible stories to the Spanish children (the Navarros had brought them for Sunday school). Ping and Carmen both grew in the Lord and faithfully attended Sunday school and church. Clif also had Bible studies with them in their home. They dedicated their lives to the Lord, and soon Ping had a job and was faithful and dependable to be at work every day, He was able to buy a car to drive to work and to use for the Lord to drive Spanish neighbors, friends, and relatives to church. (Do you see the mustard seed starting to grow and branch out?)

Ping was holding services in Spanish at the Frederiksted Baptist Sunday school building at the same time Clif was holding services in English in the church auditorium. Both groups met together during the Sunday school opening. They learned to sing choruses in both Spanish and English, and it was a great time of singing and fellowshipping together. Both Spanish and English ministries were growing, and the services were crowded. The church was near town, and people could easily walk to the service.

About the same time, a government building in Freedensburg became available to meet in for services. It was in a large Spanish village where Ping's mother, father, and other family members lived. Spanish services were started there and were well-attended. The Spanish people who were in the Frederiksted Baptist Church moved to the new church.

Through Ping's changed life and preaching of the Word, his parents and many in his family and the Spanish village came to know the Lord as their Savior. Offerings were taken and saved toward the purchase of land in the area of Clifton Hill, Christiansted, to build a Spanish Baptist church. The Baptist General Conference (BGC) of Chicago helped purchase some property to build a church, for which everyone was grateful and praised the Lord.

Along with the Bible studies Clif was having, Ping also took a correspondence Bible study course from a Baptist seminary in Costa Rica. He received a graduation diploma in 1965. Ping was preaching, and God called him to be ordained into the ministry. The ordination for Gaspar (Ping) Navarro was held on May 12, 1969, at the Frederiksted Baptist Church on St. Croix. Clif and other Baptist pastors and missionaries officiated in the ordination service.

After several years, a beautiful Spanish Baptist church building was completed on the Clifton Hill property. It was the first Spanish Baptist church of Clifton Hill, St.

Croix, built by Pastor Gaspar Navarro, his son, Jose, and some members. On May 7, 1971, Clif married Carmen and Ping's son, Jose Navarro, and their daughter Rosa Navarro, in a double wedding ceremony at the Frederiksted Baptist Church.

In 1978, Jose Navarro attended the Spanish Baptist General Conference Seminary in Chicago. At the time, Jose had four children. In 1982, he graduated with a four-year diploma and was ordained into the ministry. While studying, Jose assisted the pastor of the Lafaa Baptist Church in Waukegan, Illinois. After graduation, Jose returned to St. Croix and assisted his father for one year at the Spanish Baptist church of Clifton Hill.

Reverend Don Dye with the BGC Home Missions in Florida encouraged Jose to start a Baptist church in Tampa. Jose joined with the English speaking Concord Baptist church. He started Spanish services and was pastor there for twenty years. Jose returned to St. Croix in the summer of 2005 to plant another Spanish Baptist church.

On August 26, 2001, on their fiftieth wedding anniversary, Clif renewed the marriage vows of Pastor Gaspar and Mrs. Carmen Navarro in Tampa, Florida. We thank God for the courage Carmen had before she became a Christian to ask her neighbor to drive her and her children to church in their station wagon. Back in that time period, Catholics were not allowed to visit other churches.

It made us realize that we can never speak to the wrong person about Jesus, nor can we invite the wrong person to church to hear a gospel message, even though they may not speak or understand another language.

The Navarro family moved in God's direction because

Carmen sought after God. Sometimes, it takes the wife to step out for God and fervently pray for her husband and family. Ping was saved soon after the encounter with Clif at the bar in Frederiksted.

The Navarro's son and daughter, a number of relatives, friends, and many Puerto Rican families came to know the Lord as their Savior. And a Spanish Baptist church was planted and built by the Navarros. What started as small as a mustard seed had become a huge tree where others could take refuge. It started by saying yes to Jesus and His will. Not only did God reach out to the Spanish community, He also wanted to reach the children of St. Croix, and He gave us a dream in our hearts to do so.

Pastor and Mrs. Navarro, Jose and Carmen, and family

How We Began Carib Youth Camp

It only takes a spark to get a fire going, and soon all those around can warm up in its glowing; that's how it is with God's love, once you've experienced it, you spread the love to everyone, you want to pass it on.

—"Pass It On," an old Christian campfire song

Many of you reading might have fond memories of the way that a Christian camp changed your hearts and lives. My life was changed at a Christian youth camp in Michigan. We also saw God work strongly at the Camp of the Suwannee River, where Clif and I worked for a time. God laid it on our hearts to give the children of St. Croix the opportunity to attend a Christian camp where they could learn about Jesus, and so the first step was for us to pray for His help in the form of some camp property.

Now sometimes, it is necessary to put some feet to prayer, and in this case, we went out scouting for a suitable place for a Christian camp. We climbed hills and looked about and finally found a beautiful spot on a hillside overlooking the sparkling Caribbean. The man who owned the property said that we could have it for our youth camp, but after hiking down the steep hill in the heat of the sun, bathing in our clothes to cool off, and hauling baby Mark with us back up the hill, the place wasn't as appealing. We realized that although it was beautiful, it wouldn't be a wise choice for us. Materials and food and water would all have to be carried up and down the hill by foot, enough supplies for up to twenty-five campers. And it was impossible to get a car down into the area.

After some more searching, we found another beautiful camp location at Davis Beach, and the property was loaned to us. It had some old stone building ruins on it that were once used for slave quarters, but now this property was going to be used to set people free from the sin that bound them.

Our first camping experience at Davis Beach was great. The Boy Scout organization had been kind enough to loan us pup tents. We had recruited about twenty campers from the streets of Frederiksted; we asked them while they were out playing if they would like to attend camp. Most of them said yes and would take us to their homes so we could meet their parents and get their permission. That is how Carib Camp got started, and it has been a blessing and changed many lives over the years. When you dare to say yes to God, He keeps giving you dreams and ways to make them come about. And He keeps helping you to touch yet more people. Here are some Carib Camp stories I want to share with you:

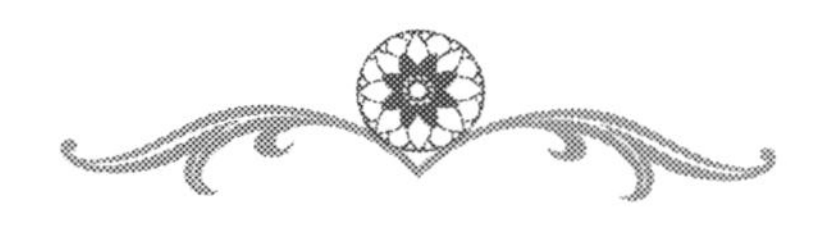

Carib Youth Camp: Where Even the Food is an Adventure

> Yonder is the sea, great and wide, in which
> are swarms of innumerable creeping things,
> creatures both small and great.

Turtles are awesome creatures that can weigh up to two hundred pounds. Turtles have a small but highly developed brain, with keen senses of vision, smell, and equilibrium. Turtles have thick moveable eyelids to protect their eyes, and they are able to discriminate forms and colors and detect the smell of ripe fruit from quite a distance. Turtles make their home on earth and in oceans where the climate is warm. Their bony shells protect both their back and underside, and they can pull their head, neck, legs, and tail in under the shell. God has created very cool creatures, and the turtle is one that has universal appeal.

On St. Croix in the nineteen fifties, turtles had an appeal that had little to do with the fact that they are such neat animals. The turtle appeal was for the way they cooked up and satisfied hungry stomachs. There were no laws to protect them from being hunted, and so there were many recipes for turtle floating around back then.

Once, a friend told us some turtle tales that aroused our curiosity. He said that one night out on the beach under a full moon, he saw a huge turtle swimming toward him with a head that was larger than his own. He suggested that tonight would be the perfect night to spot such turtles, as there was a full moon. My mother agreed to watch baby Mark, so Clif and I could go to the beach, in hopes of glimpsing a huge sea turtle.

We arrived on the edge of the beach and found a place to view unobtrusively through assorted tropical grape bushes and palm trees. The bushes seemed alive that night with creatures rustling about. Possibly there were mongooses, lizards, or rats. The full moon had the same effect as a floodlight and illuminated the sandy white beach. Our friend kept panning the beach in search of a big turtle, and we followed suit.

Suddenly, he said, "Shhh! I think I see a big turtle. Stay here while I go closer to be sure that's what it is."

He ventured onto the beach and then hurried back to summon us. I had never seen such a huge turtle in all of my life.

Needless to say, island sensibilities were such that the turtle was caught and brought to our house about four o'clock in the morning. It provided plenty of meat that was used for feeding the young people at Carib Camp and to share with the church members at Frederiksted Baptist Church. The turtle also had about four hundred twenty eggs inside, which made almost a pail full of egg yolks, which were not allowed to go to waste. Turtle eggs were scrambled for breakfasts and worked into recipes and stews. Turtle eggs are sort of tough and stretchy, like cheese on pizza. We learned that God can even use a turtle to bless us as it provided an abundance of food for many people.

Keep an open mind about what you may be eating on the mission field.

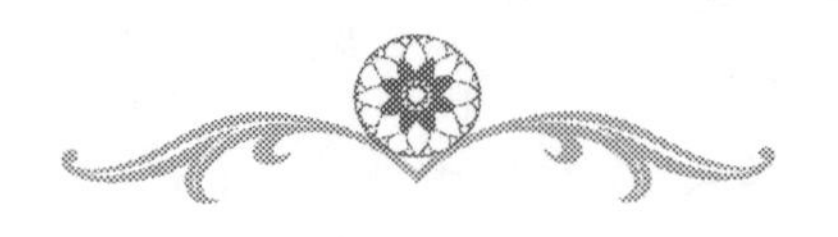

Divine Timing

Now listen, you who say, 'Today or tomorrow we will go to this or that city, spend a year there, carry on business and make money.' Why, you do not even know what will happen tomorrow. What is your life? You are a mist that appears for a little while and then vanishes.

In God's infinite love, He has a plan for each of us. This is clear as I tell you about a young teenager. Children were playing in the street, and we would ask them if they would like to attend Carib Camp for a week. A young boy and his twin sister spoke up: "We wanna go!"

We followed them to their house and explained to their mother that Carib Camp was a Christian youth camp, a branch of the Frederiksted Baptist Church, where Clif was pastor. We asked her if the young boy and his sister could go to the camp for a week. They were so happy when their mother said yes.

Monday morning, we picked up the two of them at their house. Young Teenager and Young Boy, eleven years old at the time, climbed into our Volkswagen bus, each carrying a paper bag with their clothes for the week at Carib Camp. It was a fun-filled week with games, hikes, swimming, crafts, and challenging Bible lessons and food. The fee for each child was $4, and some couldn't pay.

Norill Gumbs was from Anguilla. He was a student at the Blue Water Bible College on St. Thomas. When college was out for the summer, Norill came to St. Croix to live with us and to help us at Carib Camp. Norill was a clown with the kids. He could run with a glass of water on his head and kids chasing him, and not spill a drop.

On Friday afternoon, our Volkswagen bus was loaded with Carib Campers. Laughter and excitement filled the bus as Clif drove them from Carib Camp to Ham's Bluff at the northwest end of St. Croix. All week long, the campers had anticipated the hike up the long, steep hill to the lighthouse. They were anxious to explore the lighthouse tower, as it unceasingly shines light to guide ships in the Caribbean.

It's interesting to note that lighthouses don't ring bells or fire guns to call attention to their light; they just shine.

Norill led the hike up the hill to the lighthouse. Temperatures were in the nineties, but it didn't bother Norill or the kids. They knew when they returned from the hike they would swim in the Caribbean Sea and eat juicy mangos that we had gathered from mango trees in the forest before the hike.

Young Boy was one of the first campers off the bus, running towards the trail to the lighthouse, but Young Teenager lingered behind. She was the last girl off the bus. She said she had an awful headache and asked me if she could have an aspirin; she wanted to stay with me and not go on the hike. I remembered that the first day of camp, Young Teenager had given me a note from her mother and some aspirin. The note said, "Sometimes Young Teenager has headaches. The doctor ordered aspirin whenever she has a headache at camp." Several times during the week, Young Teenager had asked me for aspirin. Sometimes, she sat on the sidelines and watched the campers play ball and take part in other activities. Perhaps hearing their laughter and seeing their joy helped to distract her from some of her headache pain.

I gave her an aspirin, and we moved to the shade under a coconut palm tree, where we sat in the sand and talked about Jesus and the Bible. It was an opportunity to share Jesus with Young Teenager and to make sure she understood God's plan of salvation. It was God's perfect timing with an hour of quiet time to talk while the campers were at the lighthouse. That afternoon, Young Teenager prayed to Jesus and asked him to save her.

Friday evening, Carib Campers gathered around the campfire singing choruses and giving testimonies of some of the great things God had done for them that week at camp. It was exciting to hear some of the campers share that they had accepted Jesus Christ as their personal Savior during that week at camp.

Young Teenager thanked the Lord for saving her. She said she learned that Jesus loved her, and she loved the song, "With Jesus in the family – happy, happy home." She came from a large family with many brothers and sisters, and she wished they could all come to Carib Camp too. Her father was an atheist, and her mother was a Catholic but didn't think she had time to go to church with so many children. Perhaps Young Teenager wished Jesus was in her family and that it would have made her home a "happy, happy home," like the song she learned at Carib Camp.

Saturday afternoon, the Carib Campers loaded into our Volkswagen bus, and we delivered them to their homes. They were so sad that the week at camp had ended. It had gone by so quickly.

On Sunday morning, many of the campers came to Sunday school at the Frederiksted Baptist Church, but we missed Young Teenager. Young Boy told us his sister had to stay home. The next Sunday, Young Boy came back to Sunday school without his twin sister again.

He said, "The doctor sent Young Teenager to Puerto Rico to see a specialist. The doctor operated and removed a tumor from inside her head."

We visited their mother. She told us that she was at Young Teenager's bedside in the hospital in Puerto Rico and as she came out of the anesthesia, she opened her eyes and started to sing the little chorus she had learned at Carib Camp: "With Jesus in the family." Then she closed her eyes and never opened them again. Her mother said the little song was the last thing she heard her daughter say.

Little had I realized it would be Young Teenager's last week at Carib Camp and the last time we would ever see her here on earth. God took her home to heaven to be with Him.

God prepared Young Teenager for her new home in heaven before she passed away. I thank God for the opportunity to share Jesus and the plan of salvation with her. The day of the lighthouse hike was God's plan for the day she accepted Jesus Christ as her Savior.

If you are not already saved, God has a plan for you to be saved. We must be ready to meet the Lord in case of an unexpected early departure (death). God is ready to save you. Ask Jesus to forgive your sin and become your Savior.

God, in His divine timing, led us to another person at Carib Camp, this time a peculiar old man who camped year round and needed to know about Jesus.

The Old Man Who Lived in a Tree

The Lord does not look at the things man looks at. Man looks at the outward appearance, but the Lord looks at the heart.

Remember the story of the old woman who lived in a shoe? This is the story of an old man who lived in a tree.

Each week at Carib Camp, we had a new group of boys and girls. Clif and I took them on hikes. When we were hiking through thick bushes and trees, we felt like we were in the jungles of a little Africa. There were coconut, mango, and locust trees and lots of green vines hanging everywhere. The vines were strong enough that the kids could grab them and swing back and forth.

One day, we were hiking on a winding dirt road near Carib Camp when we heard a rustling noise in the bushes near the creek. The boys and girls were curious to see what the rustling noise was, so they rushed over the little hilltop searching all over the area.

Suddenly, an old man stuck his head out and said loudly, "Hel-LOOoooo!" Some of his front teeth were missing, his hair was wild and unkept, his eyes were like glassy black marbles, his beard was long and bushy, his pants were ragged and dirty, and he had no shirt on. He was living in a tree.

By that time, all the campers were screaming and hanging onto us. How would you like to get acquainted with a person who lived in a tree back in the bush? Well, you know what? We did. Clif and I went back later to visit him. He told us he grew provisions – vegetables, like cassava, plantain, and yams. He also grew a plant that had big elephant ears; he cooked the root of the plant in an old charcoal pot, and he ate the root. He watered his garden with creek water, using an old rusty can to carry the water to the plants. He ate locusts and coconuts, mangos, and papayas from the local trees.

Remember in the Bible that John the Baptist ate locusts and wild honey? Well, we also picked some locusts and ate them. I even brought a locust pod back from St. Croix Island to show people in the States.

The man told us he used the creek for everything. He drank it and bathed in it. We also saw a wild pig wallowing in the mud and bathing in the same creek water. (Ugh!)

He also told us that he saw flying lights with tails flying back and forth at night. He thought that they were evil spirits trying to get him. He told us that someone was doing witchcraft on him and that he was scared.

Clif told him that Jesus loved him, died on the cross for him, and wanted to come into his heart and give him a new life. He said that Jesus would change his heart and forgive his sin and make him a new person, a new man. He told the man he would have peace of mind if he would pray to Jesus and not listen to the devil. Clif read the Bible to him, specifically Romans 10:13: "For whosoever shall call upon the name of the Lord shall be saved." The man prayed and asked Jesus to forgive his sins and wash them away.

Do you think God heard his prayer? Yes, and all of heaven rejoiced. Can we ever tell the wrong person about Jesus? No, God's will is for everyone to have eternal life through Jesus. Everyone, including the campers, rejoiced over the old man's decision for salvation.

Carmen Navarro cooked Spanish food for Carib Camp. Every day at lunchtime, one of the campers carried a plate of food to the old man who lived in the tree. We wanted him to know that God loved him, and so did we. He began to have a smile on his face; he looked happier, and indeed, he was happier. God made a difference in his life.

Everyone rejoiced about the day we were hiking and heard the rustling noise in the bush that brought attention to the old man living in the tree. A soul was found for Jesus.

You might think this story was unusual, but think again. Long before this ever happened, the call of Jesus came to another man who was in a tree: Zacchaeus. You can find opportunities to witness everywhere; souls are in the strangest places. Keep your eyes peeled and your feet shod with the gospel of peace.

While the old man was content as could be in his tree, most people really do desire a bit more in a building structure. And so build we did.

Building Lives and Structures

Every man's work shall be made manifest: for the day shall declare it, because it shall be revealed by fire; and the fire shall try every man's work of what sort it is.
—1 Corinthians 3:13

The Bible tells us to be careful how we build because it will be tested by fire to see what kind of work it is. We were careful to keep Jesus as our foundation and to build with quality in everything that we put our hands to. We built with love as we reached out to people; as the need for a church grew, we built physical structures with God's love too. Clif always said anything worth doing is worth doing right, and our work reflected that kind of an attitude at every turn.

Out of an old ruin in the village of Hugensburg, lives were made new by the saving grace of God as Clif preached the gospel in the open-air meetings. The Holy Spirit drew the people to come, and we believe that the music we played helped, as well. Clif played the trumpet, and I played the accordion.

Soon, the meetings were moved to Frederiksted, where

we rented an old wooden house for $52 a month. We made a model church from a cement block and placed it on a table for special offerings towards the building fund. People gave, sacrificially. Mrs. Henry, a Crucian member in her sixties, made coconut candy and walked the streets of Frederiksted to sell it from a straw basket; she faithfully gave her tithes and offerings every week to the church.

We searched up and down the streets of Frederiksted, looking for property. A man said, "If you find land, let me know. I'd like some land to build a bar." But we wanted to build a church where people would never thirst again. We found an acre right next to the house where we held services. It was overgrown with bushes and trees. It seems God kept it hidden for us. It was in the corner of town and on a good road, the perfect location for the first Baptist church on St. Croix.

Around this time, an elderly man became very ill and was hospitalized, and we were called upon by the family to help care for him. We took turns staying with him in the hospital. When he recovered, he gave us an envelope with money in it.

We said, "No, what we did to help was our part of serving the Lord."

Later, we learned that this man was the owner of the property next to our meeting place. When the man and his two brothers were deciding the price of the land, they were very sympathetic towards us for helping their father. They set the price at $1,400, which was a very reasonable price for an acre of land in Frederiksted. The church offerings were saved over a period of time, mainly pennies, nickels, dimes, and quarters. This covered the amount except for eighty cents. It was quite a boost of faith for the congregation and for us.

God continually led and directed us in the building of the first Baptist church on the island. Fill dirt was needed for the side of the hill to level the land. God provided it at just the right time: A bulldozer began digging a cistern nearby for the new post office and needed a place to get rid of the dirt. Guess what? Truckload after truckload of dirt was dumped on our church property to level the land. After leveling, Clif went back to tell them we had all the dirt we needed. Their answer was, "That was our last load; no more!" The rock quarry gave us all the blue rock we needed to build the retaining walls in front and the side of the hill. Clif, Dad Lyons, and I handpicked truckloads of blue rock and loaded it into our pickup truck to build rock walls. Each day, we'd say, "We wonder what God will do today?" It was amazing how God supplied, but then again, He owns it all anyway.

Church plans were drawn by Tony Hougerhyde, a member of the Bethel Baptist Church in Bradenton, Florida, at no charge. Clif worked on the building while holding services in the rented house. Several local people laid blocks. Ray Thompson from Blue Water Bible College in St. Thomas helped Clif put the roof on. Many Stateside people prayed and gave as the church was being planted.

People were hearing the gospel, and the congregation was growing. We were thrilled and excited to be pioneering a new work. It was a learning experience. We learned as we went along that it was hard work. We learned from the postage stamp slogan, "Stick to the Job" until the job is finished. We realized what a great God we served. Finally, a Baptist church was built (born), the very first Baptist church on St. Croix. Some people on the island had never seen a Baptist church before.

A man who had been watching the church being built noticed the large cement tank inside the front of the church (our future baptismal tank); he asked if that was where Clif was going to preach.

The day finally arrived. The congregation moved to their new church home, the Frederiksted Baptist Church. The church was dedicated on January 23, 1964. Reverend and Mrs. Gordon Anderson brought greetings from the Baptist General Conference of Chicago. Reverend Anderson gave a challenging message to the church. Many Stateside Baptist General Conference churches prayed and supported the work, especially our home church, Bethel Baptist Church of Bradenton. After the completion and establishment of the church, we enjoyed a three-month furlough to the States after being relieved by Pastor Arthur and Ruth Westerhoff. They were welcomed by everyone.

Reverend and Mrs. Guy Rainwater brought greetings and encouraging words from the Eastside Baptist Church in Atlanta. They had supported us as missionaries to St. Croix since 1956. The governor of the Virgin Islands, Ralph M. Paiewonsky, and his wife attended. He gave a heart stirring charge to the church and afterwards invited us and our parents to their beautiful home on St. Croix for a tea party. There was much rejoicing over the newly completed church building, and the great attendance.

New people were coming to know the Lord as their Savior and were being baptized and joined the church. Praise God, the mortgage was soon paid off, as well. In the meantime, God was leading Clif to reach out and build a Baptist church near the Sunny Isle area. Mr. and Mrs. Ludvig Johansen, Sr., members of the Frederiksted Baptist Church, donated one and a half acres in the Sunny Isle area, the very location that Clif had in mind to build another Baptist church.

It was heart-rending to us to leave the congregation we loved. The people were equally saddened. Clif shared with the congregation his conviction that the Lord was directing him to take a huge step of faith and plant another Baptist church. Clif resigned from the Frederiksted Baptist Church on June 20, 1970, in order to devote his time to building the Sunny Isle Baptist Church. Clif and I departed with the blessing of the congregation. In addition, the church generously donated $9,000 toward the building fund to build the second Baptist church on the island. Praise God for his blessings.

In the meantime, God was preparing a student at Blue Water Bible College on St. Thomas for a ministry on St. Croix. The Frederiksted Baptist Church called Wilfred Richards to be pastor. Following Pastor and Mrs. Richards, Pastor and Mrs. Frank Rogers, also graduates of Blue Water Bible College, ministered at the Frederiksted Baptist Church for many years until God called Frank Rogers to his heavenly home.

Between the transition and the search for a pastor, Deacon Randolph Pascal faithfully filled the pulpit until God sent a pastor. The Gilbert family were members of the Frederiksted Baptist Church in the early 1960s while we were serving as missionaries at the church. After we left Frederiksted Baptist Church to plant another church on St. Croix, John Gilbert and his brother attended Bible College in Texas. They graduated, married, and became

Baptist pastors. The Frederiksted Baptist Church called John Gilbert to be their pastor.

The Gilberts invited us to St. Croix for the forty-third anniversary of the Frederiksted Baptist Church on January 29, 2006, and paid for our airline tickets. Clif was honored to be the guest speaker, and the church was full and running over. It was thrilling to see God's blessings on the first church we built back in the sixties and that it was still going strong. Pastor and Mrs. Gilbert have been doing a great work at the church since 2005. How good it is to see young people grow up in the church, go to Bible college, and dare to say yes to God, serving Him wherever He leads them. The Frederiksted Baptist Church provides a house for the homeless at Whim, as well as spiritual and physical food. The church also has an outreach program for children, helping them with homework after school and teaching them computer skills. Pastor and Mrs. John Gilbert have touched so many lives with their hearts of love.

This is a lot of history here, I know, but all started with daring to say yes to God. Open up your life to God, and life will open up to you.

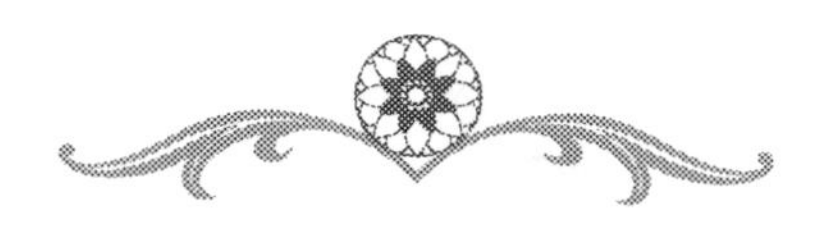

The Missing Piece

"Commit thy works unto the Lord and
thy thoughts shall be established."
Proverbs 16:3

Today's generations want the same things that the generations preceding them wanted: success. They want success in their relationships, success in their ministry endeavors, success in their careers. They are in awe when they hear that a couple is celebrating their fiftieth wedding anniversary, they are amazed at the stories of hard times endured by many missionaries, and they marvel at the success and reach of some of the existing ministries today. And then they inevitably wonder, why doesn't my life look like that? They wonder, after trying hard, what some people know that they don't know or what must be so special and different about others.

The piece that is often missing today is commitment. Not much emphasis is placed on that word anymore. Trying hard isn't the same as commitment, but this generation often errors in interchanging the two terms. Trying hard is a good thing, but commitment will make all the difference in the world. Real commitment is more than just trying hard. Commitment won't let you give up. It stays the course against all odds.

Clif and I tried hard in our ministry, but if that was all that we did, we wouldn't have made it for thirty-six years as missionaries to St. Croix. We made a commitment to God, not a promise to try hard, but a rock-solid commitment when we said yes to God.

What held our marriage together was not only love but commitment. What brought this book to pass was commitment.

Years before I even thought of writing this book, an evangelist named Pastor Amato came to our church in St. Croix and laid his hands on Clif in front of the whole congregation; he blessed him and then turned to where I was seated by the organ and did something quite profound that shaped my destiny.

He said to me in front of the whole congregation, "LeEllen, I want you to promise me something: I want you to commit in front of everyone gathered here today to write a book telling about the miracles of God's work here on St. Croix. I want you to promise me and commit that you will write it down in a book so it won't be forgotten. Others deserve to be told about God's work here."

He urged me to make a commitment in front of God and the entire congregation. Commitment is a strong force. It could be what keeps you on track, when the going gets hard or when there are things that look like a lot more fun that you could be doing.

I challenge you today to not only dare to say yes to God but commit to saying yes to God and to whatever His plan is for your life. Don't just try to follow Him, commit to following Him, at whatever cost.

Commitment could be the missing piece that will make your life come together into a beautiful picture that glorifies God. It's a free choice that will cost you everything. We are glad we made and kept our commitments, because in keeping them, there has been great reward, more than what we can ever capture and record on the pages of this book. The rewards have outweighed the sacrifices by far. Commitment is not always easy to find these days, but I do know of a good example of something that was very committed bothering us, and very good at it too.

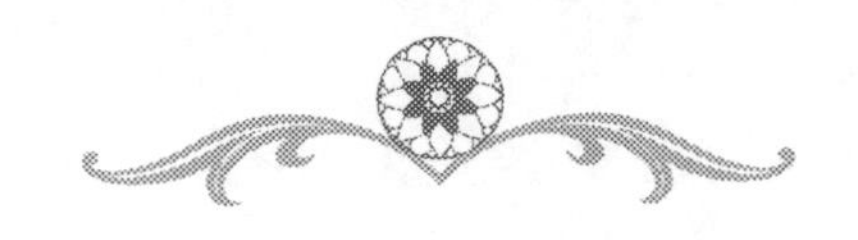

Church Pigeon

"Not forsaking the assembling of ourselves together, as the manner of some is; but exhorting one another: and so much the more, as ye see the day approaching." Hebrews 10:25

In 1989, Hurricane Hugo devastated St. Croix with torrential rains and winds more than 150 miles per hour; winds blew away buildings and their roofs, knocked down trees and telephone poles, and cut phones, water, and power for weeks.

Now, a little further back than 1989, in the days of Noah, after the devastation of the flood, Noah sent out a dove to see if there was any dry land. As long as the dove couldn't find a better deal than the food available at the ark, it came back to roost where it knew it could find provisions. Well, directly after Hurricane Hugo, a pigeon found that our church had the best provisions around. The church became a type of ark for him in a sea of people scrambling to recover. Hurricane Hugo was tough on animals, insects, and birds, and they were scarce after the storm, but at least one bird could be sighted each day, presiding faithfully over the entrance of Southgate Baptist Church and the food tables directly below. We had tables of FEMA food and water set up just outside of the church entrance to distribute to people in need as they lined up to receive a ration of food and water.

While our new friend sported an ID bracelet on his ankle and found people-watching absolutely fascinating, he simply didn't have good social graces. Pigeon soon made a nuisance of himself by garnishing the tables below with his droppings. At first, we tried to work with Pigeon by simply moving him to a less consequential place to perch, but to no avail. Like people, Pigeon had preferences, and he clearly asserted that his favorite perch was over the church entrance door. Even if the food tables were moved elsewhere, Pigeon would have made a fine mess of the church entrance door area.

Days passed, and no one showed up to claim Pigeon and relocate him. One day, our son, a young man of action, caught Pigeon and placed him in a box for transport. We kindly chauffeured Pigeon about ten miles away to the north side of the island, generously offering him new territory by the Altona Baptist Church. We paused to watch Pigeon flap his wings as he soared gracefully into the sky that loomed over what was to be his new home. With the satisfaction of a mission accomplished, we got in the truck and headed back to Southgate Baptist Church. It seems great minds do think alike, because when we arrived, there was Pigeon, sitting steadfast and immovable on his favorite perch above the entrance door and the food tables. Pigeon's church attendance was exemplary.

The next morning, Mark caught Pigeon again, and this time, we chauffeured him twenty miles away to the west end of the island. Mark released Pigeon near the Frederiksted Baptist Church, hoping he would be willing to change membership. Pigeon shot up into the sky in sheer joy and made quick friends with one and then two other birds, as they all soared higher. We were so happy for Pigeon that he had been able to find some little companions so fast so that he wouldn't feel alone in his new surroundings. With a sense of relief, Mark and I climbed back into our truck, content that we had gone the extra mile to help our feathered friend.

However, Pigeon valued commitment and church attendance beyond what we would have expected of him, and by the next morning, we saw him perched steadfast and immovable on his favorite perch above the food tables. Pigeon's determination caught people's interest, and soon "pigeon talk" spread across the island (although phone service was out). He was not just Pigeon anymore; he was now known as the Church Pigeon due to his strong affiliation with us. Church Pigeon finally stopped returning to our ark of FEMA food provisions when a man who raised pigeons heard about his exploits and immediately recognized with great interest that Church Pigeon was, in fact, a homing pigeon. He was delighted to take him to his pigeon farm on the east end of the island. We presume Church Pigeon has been rewarded with a full life suitable for such a faithful bird, one flocked with pigeon friends and relatives and ample flying opportunities. We must admit that we were very delighted that Church Pigeon was no longer present at the church and was no longer making numerous contributions to the food tables and ground below.

"Not forsaking the assembling of ourselves together, as the manner of some is; but exhorting one another: and so much the more, as ye see the day approaching" (Hebrews 10:25).

Don't let a pigeon be found more faithful than you.

The next story is about a woman who could achieve so much in different areas of her life because of her commitment to Jesus and to being faithful:

South Gate pigeon and his shadow

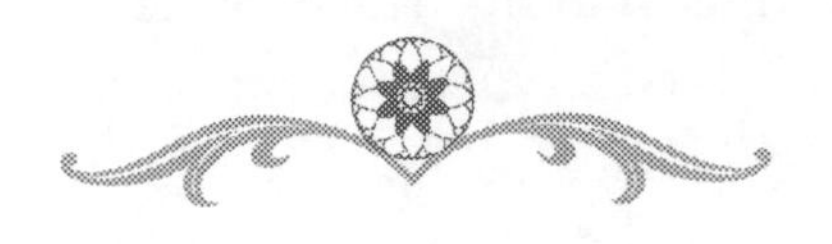

Peaches

"Seest thou a man diligent in his business?
He shall stand before kings, he shall not stand
before mean men." Proverbs 22:29

This is the story of Peaches Dixon, who has a servant's heart and is known for her faithfulness and diligence.

Clif and I were visiting Grove Place, a small village of about nine hundred people. We were going door-to-door in the village, sharing tracts that explained the gospel to people. One of the tracts that we handed out was "How to Get to Heaven from St. Croix." We also gave invitations to visit our church.

We knocked on the door of a humble little dwelling, and a friendly lady came to the door. She spoke English with a British accent and had come from the island of St. Kitts to find work. This was while my parents had moved from Florida to live next to us in St. Croix. My mom hired Peaches to help her with housework.

Peaches helped us too. She said, "I'll work three days and give two days free because you are missionaries." This was even before Peaches made a commitment to Jesus. God has honored and blessed Peach's generous heart all through the years.

My mom had a missionary heart too, and one day, she

fixed Peaches eight sandwiches to eat while she talked to her about the Bible and Jesus. Peaches chuckles as she recalls this. You've heard of building bridges to reach the lost, but how about making sandwiches to reach them? My mom earned the right to share the gospel with Peaches through sandwiches and friendship.

In 1956, Peaches made a commitment and accepted Jesus while Reverend Rainwater from Eastside Baptist Church in Atlanta was in St. Croix, conducting evangelistic meetings. He and his wife had come down to be a part of the dedication of our first church. A little later, wedding bells were ringing at the Frederiksted Baptist Church, where Clif married Peaches and Joseph, and she changed her last name from Dixon to Simmonds.

During the 1960s, Peaches and Joseph took jobs with a large company. Joseph worked at the company, and Peaches worked at the motel. Peaches' work included preparing breakfast for Mr. Washington and other officials while they were on the island; Mr. Washington talked to her like she was one of the family. He was of a different belief, and Peaches was a Christian, but she still invited him to all the special programs at the church that involved the Junior Choir, which Peaches directed.

Peaches went the extra mile with the choir, working with them tirelessly on weekends to rehearse their parts and shuttled them about in her station wagon or the church van. She even bought yards of new material with her own money so each girl in the choir could have a beautiful new dress to wear. Mrs. Decallie, a seamstress, sewed all the dresses. Peaches also provided for each of the boys in the choir with new white shirts. Every program that Peaches and the choir presented was well organized and practiced until every song was perfected memorized. Wow. Anyone would love to have Peaches and her Junior Choir at their church.

Once when we were on furlough in the States, we saw a presentation of a living Christmas tree. We were so impressed that we brought back a tape with the program and the plans on paper to build the staging for our own church's Living Christmas Tree. Clif, George Decallie, and several other men constructed a stage that stood about sixteen feet tall, with room for thirty-five youth to stand in, while singing and presenting the story of Jesus.

Peaches was up to the challenge and groomed the Junior Choir to give a wonderful performance for our first Living Christmas Tree presentation in St. Croix. The program was repeated several times during the Christmas season and in the following years; it drew a crowd, making an impact as it relayed the beautiful story of the birth of Jesus.

Peaches not only worked hard at the company and with the Junior Choir, she also raised five children. She had been considering sending her children to her mother on St. Kitts Island so she would be more free to work on St. Croix. This is a common and accepted economic strategy with islanders, and in return, some of the money they earn is sent to the grandparents to help raise the children. She told me she was considering this, and I shared with her what the Bible says in Proverbs 22:6: "Train up a child in the way he should go, and when he is old, he will not depart from it." We shared with Peaches how important it is to take responsibility to raise and train up children in the Lord. Peaches prayed about all of this and decided it was important to teach her children in her own home.

All five of her children were raised up in the church where Peaches received Jesus as her Savior, and all have been saved and baptized and are active members. Peaches is now in her sixties and is still working at the company and leading the Junior Choir. Her picture hangs proudly on the wall at the company, and she is well-liked by everyone. She's always willing to help and give to others. She has a good attitude and is happy and pleasant to get along with. She has been given larger housing quarters on the company property in a nice place that is fenced in for security.

Peaches dared to say yes to God when she accepted Jesus as her Savior. She didn't wait until she somehow became perfect but dived right in serving the One who is perfect. Two of her children, Marcella and Bertha, graduated from Bethel College in St. Paul, Minnesota; Leon and Norma graduated from Florida colleges; Juneau, her youngest son, served our country in the Armed Forces. He served in Vietnam and in Iraq, where he received third degree burns. We appreciate the sacrifice he made to protect our country.

Peaches came to St. Croix looking for work, and little did she know that the Lord had so much important work for her to do. As Peaches was diligent and worked hard, the Lord put her in positions of responsibility, working directly with Mr. Washington and other officials, as well as leading the Junior Choir at the Sunny Isle Baptist Church. The Lord has vast harvest fields and has useful work for every believer to do, regardless of age or ability. Find a way to serve God and be faithful, even if it is being faithful in prayer for those in ministry or cooking meals for someone.

Now the world and the island of St. Croix have changed much. After forty years, the large company made a drastic move and shut down production. Due to a bad economy, several stores and tourist shops have closed also.

Peaches Simmonds, director, Living Christmas Tree

A Dangerous Encounter

Surely He shall deliver you from the snare of the fowler.
—Psalm 91:3

One Sunday afternoon, Peaches was practicing with the youth for the program they were going to put on that evening at Sunny Isle Baptist Church. Clif and I were at the church early when the phone rang. It was Sarah Marks, a dear elderly member of the church who needed a ride to the service. I volunteered to pick her up, and a couple of the young people volunteered to go with me. We climbed into the car, with Aggie sitting in the front and Young Teenager in the back.

Imagine three young ladies riding down Centerline Road on St. Croix when all of a sudden, a shiny, black car appeared to be following close behind us, blowing its horn.

I looked in my rearview mirror and said, "It looks like a police car."

I looked at my speedometer but I was only going twenty-five miles per hour, which was definitely under the speed limit. The car behind us kept blowing his horn, so I slowed down and pulled over to the side of the road.

A policeman got out of his car and walked over to

my window. He asked, "Ma'am, do you have a driver's license?" and when I replied yes, he asked to see it.

As I reached for my billfold in my purse on the floor to show him my license, Aggie whispered, "No! Don't show him because he isn't wearing a badge or a uniform. That man is not a policeman."

God allowed Aggie to detect that the man was an imposter and up to no good. I immediately stepped on the gas and took off down the road, leaving the man stunned as he stood on the roadside.

We later learned that the elderly lady we were on our way to pick up that day, Sarah Marks, was a faithful prayer warrior in her eighties who covered us in prayer three times a day. God honored her prayers and kept us safe through the years of ministering on St. Croix.

When Sister Marks heard about the incident, she said, "That man thought he had easy prey with three girls in the car, but what he didn't realize was their guardian angel was riding in the car with them, watching o'er."

The man's plan to snatch my billfold while pretending to be a policeman requesting a driver's license was deterred by prayer. Sister Marks continued to pray for God's protecting hand upon us; she had been praying that afternoon for us while waiting for her ride to church.

We thank God for prayer warriors and our guardian angel watching over us and protecting us. Sister Marks, being an octogenarian, could have easily contented herself that she was already doing her part in faithfully praying for us, but she looked for other ways to bless us as well, and boy, did she.

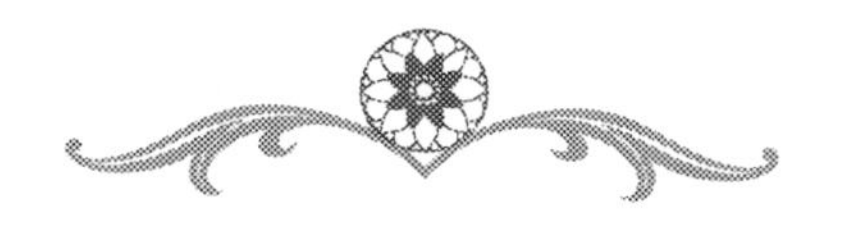

Labor of Love

And every one that hath forsaken houses, or brethren, or sisters or father or mother, or wife or children or lands for my names sake, shall receive an hundred fold, and shall inherit the everlasting life.

—Matthew 19:29

The family of God is big and worldwide. In St. Croix, Sister Sarah Marks became like a mother to us in a faraway land. She was a prayer warrior and prayed for us and our ministry three times a day. We were so blessed with her love and prayers. When anyone in our family came down with a cold or was sick, Sister Marks always had an old-time remedy and prayed for us until we were on our feet again. She loved us and protected us. She was very protective of our son, Mark. When the girls in their teens were paying too much attention to him, she let them know that they shouldn't take advantage of the Bubars being in the ministry. Scolding them, she would say, "You should know better."

Sister Marks and her daughter Ruth Austin initiated a Labor of Love ministry for our family. They prepared Sunday dinners so we could be free to serve the Lord. Clif taught an adult class and preached in the morning and evening services. Sometimes, he held afternoon services at King's Hill, a home for the elderly. I taught the teenage class, played the organ for the Sunday school and church services, and was involved in the Sunday afternoon door-to-door visitation program. By their ministry, Ruth and Sister Marks made us more available to serve. God is so good.

Ruth did the grocery shopping and paid for it, and Sister Marks prepared and cooked the food in their home before coming to church on Sunday morning. I should add that they never missed a service. They prepared the food in pots and pans and wrapped them in foil and towels to keep everything hot.

The meals were well-balanced. About once a month, we had liver and onions, smothered in a Crucian browned onion and tomato sauce. Even Mark ate liver and onions. He liked her Crucian cooking. Another Sunday menu might be stewed goat, chicken, or duck, with rice and collard greens. There was always a fresh vegetable and a fruit drink made from tamarind tree pods or other tropical fruits. Our Sunday dinners were always delightful; this Labor of Love began early in our missionary ministry and continued for nearly twenty years.

Sometimes, when I knew we were having company, I would say, "Sister Marks, you don't need to prepare next Sunday's dinner."

She was a frail lady in her sixties but always replied, "Don't rob me of my blessing. You'll have food to eat later or tomorrow," and she'd fix the Sunday meal anyway.

She knew that Clif and Mark would be hungry after the evening service. These acts of love will always be remembered and appreciated. Sister Marks went home to receive her reward on October 13, 1989, at age ninety-five.

Clif performed her funeral service at Sunny Isle Baptist Church.

I am so thankful that God caused me to save some of Sister Marks's writings. She wrote the following letter after we had taken her and Ruth for a ride in our airplane on Thanksgiving Day:

> Dear Pastor and Sister Bubar,
>
> When we got back from our little spin in the air, I want to say in writing how much we appreciated our trip in your plane. Personally, I enjoyed it very much! I thought that was quite a treat. I praised the Lord. It was so relaxing and I enjoyed every bit of it. I saw what I could not see on the earth. The trees looked so little, the houses, the span of the ocean and the hills.
>
> You and Sister Bubar have been so nice to us as a little family, in sickness, and in many little things from the time we came to the Church in Frederiksted. I was thrilled to see our Church from the air. I was told that the folks were waving but I could not see them. We feel that you and Sister Bubar have been our own family.
>
> May God's blessing continue to pour over your hearts, souls and spirits and give you both strength and purpose to go on. I shall not cease to pray and love you. Great is our God. May God's grace, strength and His

divine power be yours as you continue to work in his vineyard for the salvation of precious souls.

Yours in His love,
Sarah and Ruth

Sister Marks also wrote us the following poem about our lives:

His Guiding Hand
By Sarah E. Marks

Great and mighty is our God.
His promises faileth never.
They who put their trust in Him
no power on earth can sever.

While in Bible college one day,
God called us to the field.
We knew not where that would be
but our lives to the Spirit did yield.

He led us to an island
way down in the Caribbean.
It was the island of St. Croix,
a place we had never seen.

We came depending on our God, Who said,
"I never will forsake
if you would break the Bread of Life
to all who will partake."

We were told when we came
no more church was needed here.
But undoubtedly we stood
for we were in God's care.

There are two towns in St. Croix:
Christiansted and Frederiksted.
The island is eighty-four square miles;
hungry souls here to be fed.

The Lord gave us a lovely son,
our little Crucian boy.
Amid the struggles and the toils,
he was our love and joy.

In process of time, a church was built
on the side of Mars Hill.
We knew that God was with us
for we were in His will.

You ask which is the greatest sin
that's committed in the island.
You'll be surprised if I should say
the greatest is religion.

The gospel of Jesus must be preached
to warn men of their sin
that they may have eternal life,
yes, a new life to begin.

Sister Marks's daughter, Ruth, requested that I go with her to the hospital to help her bring home a sweet little baby girl she adopted. She said, "Mrs. Bubar, you name her!" I chose the name Nadyne, after my sister, a missionary in Japan.

When we arrived at the hospital for the baby girl, the nurse said, "It's a baby boy."

Ruth took it so calmly. We simply changed the name to Dean, and if I remember right, the little pink baby clothes changed too. Dean has grown up to be quite a young man.

People are associated with different attributes, and while some stand out for their faithfulness and commitment, there are others that we think of and associate with determination, even a stubborn determination.

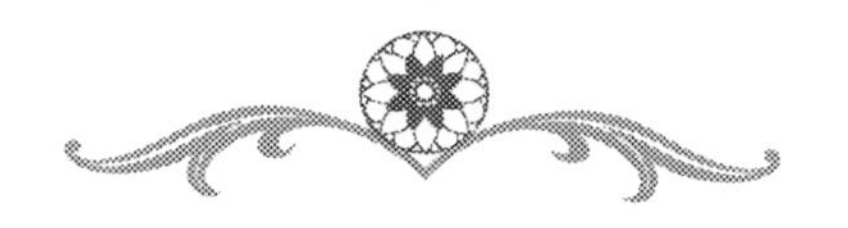

Mark's Donkey

That which is called firmness in a king
is called obstinacy in a donkey.
—John Erskine

Long before there was ever any Nike ad campaigns promoting a "Just do it" mind-set, there was our son: Mark Bubar. Even as a small child, he had a solid and abiding "Just do it" attitude. Shortly after he was born on St. Croix, Dad and Mom Lyons (my parents) left the States and moved into the house next to us. This was something quite rare for missionaries to have their parents right next door.

It was fun and exciting having my parents close by. It was also a great experience and privilege for Mark. He found out, at the ripe old age of four, just how exciting it really was.

One day, Dad Lyons came home with a pitiful-looking creature someone must have wanted to get rid of. Dad thought the price was right, five dollars, and a real bargain. He was raised on a farm in Michigan and thought kids should know how to take care of animals. So this old gray beast would be a first for Mark to learn to care for. It was appropriately named Stubborn Beast.

Young Mark was overjoyed when he saw the donkey

tied to a stake in our back yard. His little heart was filled with glee when Grandpa told him that he bought the donkey for him and that it was his very own. Unbeknownst to us, a plan was hatching in young Mark's mind.

While other four-year-olds had tricycles, Mark had a donkey. This obstinate creature was more challenging than a mere inanimate tricycle. Mark intended to make the most of his good fortune, so early one morning, I looked out our window to make sure the Stubborn Beast was still in the yard, as I routinely did each day. Sure enough he was, but there was another sight to see as well. Imagine my surprise to see our four-year-old on top of a stepladder, threatening any minute to climb onto the donkey's back.

It was a hilarious episode. Little four-year-old Mark had a determined look of concentration on his face as he prepared to step from the ladder onto a seemingly cooperative and patient donkey's back. Plans quickly went away when the mischievous old donkey relocated at the last minute, leaving Mark straddled and stretched between the donkey's back and the top of the ladder. Mark's look of concentration devolved into one of consternation.

By that time, the neighbors were peeping out of their doors and windows as we ran out to rescue our determined four-year-old before the ladder toppled over. Although Mark did not succeed at his mission, he gave us a clue as to who he was made to be. To this day, Mark still gets ideas in his mind and is not afraid to run with them. He's like the determined person on the stepladder so many years ago, only now he can build and fix things and is gifted in all kinds of practical ways. The Bible says in Proverbs that "even a child is known by his actions."

Soon after that event, another donkey appeared in our neighborhood, owned by an elderly Crucian man. His donkey and our donkey made friends and never failed to bray back and forth in their donkey language at all hours of the day and night. It didn't seem to matter that one donkey was across the road and one was in our backyard.

Unlike our donkey, which enjoyed life as a pet, the donkey across the road was a work donkey. And work he did, loaded down with bulging burlap bags of homemade charcoal, trudging along back and forth to the marketplace with the old man, along dirt roads underneath a blazing sun.

Other donkeys were hitched up to carry carts loaded down with hay, homemade charcoal, coconuts, and produce like cassavas, yams, and carrots that had been grown in various little garden patches. Market day was an everyday occurrence on St. Croix. Donkeys didn't get days off.

However, donkeys could enjoy a day of reprieve once a year in Christiansted, when a day was set aside for all kinds of fun donkey activities. Everyone and their donkeys showed up for the event. This was the only day in the year when donkey could get away with a little revenge towards their owners who worked them so hard. The donkeys took full advantage of their special day, much to everyone's delight. It was hilarious to see the donkeys attempting to race with someone on their back. The donkeys in the lead would invariably attempt to throw their riders off by suddenly applying the brakes and abruptly stopping.

I remember one donkey that was running so swiftly that he was sure to take first place, when suddenly, out of the blue, he simply stopped. No amount of coaxing could make him go even one step farther. Donkeys are some of the most stubborn and obstinate creatures on earth, next to people, perhaps.

Donkeys were also used as basic transportation and were plenteous on the roads in the 1950s, but they became somewhat obsolete as more automobiles were shipped to St. Croix. It was sad to see poor old donkeys lose their lives due to fast-driven cars; we often witnessed the remains of crashed and broken-up carts left where they had slammed violently against coconut trees along the road. Even an island cannot escape changes. St. Croix has experienced many waves of change. And then again, certain things stay the same.

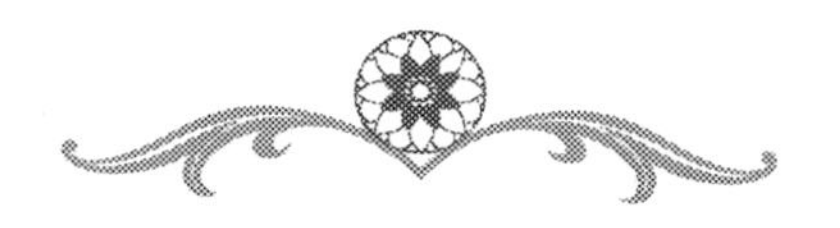

A Wishful Thought

Making the decision to have a child is momentous.
It is to decide forever to have your heart go
walking around outside of your body.
—Elizabeth Stone

Mark attended his last year of high school at the Christian Glencove Academy in Maine, while we remained in St. Croix. We missed him so much. One night during that time frame, Clif and I were praying on the way home from church. God is never too early and never too late with appointments. It was about nine o'clock as we drove home from church when we caught a glimpse of a tall blond-haired boy standing in a phone booth.

"That looks like Mark," I exclaimed.

In our wishful thinking, we hoped that somehow Mark had decided to surprise us by phoning to tell us he was on the island and wanted us to pick him up.

Clif stopped the car, and I got out with my heart pounding and slipped over to the phone booth. I could hear him talking on the phone. He had no idea anyone was near. His conversation was so intent that he didn't even notice me standing in the next booth. It turned out that it wasn't our Mark, but after he said goodbye, hung up the phone, and disappeared into the darkness, I felt the compulsion of wishful thinking.

I hurried back to our car and said, "Let's follow him." We drove down the street and around the corner, but the young man had disappeared out of sight. We continued to search and assumed he had slipped into a bar on that street.

I said, "Clif, go see if he's in there," but he elected me for the mission, since I had started it.

I went to the door of the bar, and sure enough, I saw the young man in there and beckoned for him to come out.

I introduced myself and said, "A few minutes ago, my husband and I saw you in a phone booth. You looked so much like our son, who is attending school in Maine, that we couldn't refuse the opportunity of meeting you."

He said, "My name is Bob, and I arrived in St. Croix a couple days ago."

I told him where we lived and asked if he would like to come to our home for dinner.

He said, "I would be glad to come," and told me where he was staying.

The next afternoon, Clif picked John up and brought him to our home for dinner.

It took prayer and effort to follow through with Bob to the point where we could share Christ with him. Opportunities are available as we look for them and ask God to lead us in the steps that we need to take.

We enjoyed getting to know Bob. He was a personable man in his early twenties who had grown up in the same neighborhood with an important family and had played with their kids. He conveyed that he was living life in the fast lane and tried everything. We sensed that Bob was weary and troubled and trying to escape the emptiness of that lifestyle. He thought that going to a faraway island to live would solve his problems and that all of his troubles would vanish. He even thought that living a pauper's lifestyle on the island might make him happier than his affluent lifestyle. So he left the university he had been attending, said goodbye to his family and girlfriend, and came to St. Croix in search of happiness.

That evening as we shared dinner, it was the perfect evening to share Christ with a young man far from home in a strange land. God prepared him for us and us for him. Clif opened the Bible and explained God's plan of salvation and God's love for him. For the first time in his life, Bob saw his need for Jesus. God touched his heart and life. That night, Bob prayed and asked Jesus to save him and to give him direction in his life.

God soon provided Bob with a job on the island, and he faithfully attended our church and grew in his new faith in Christ. He shared his testimony with others and began to earnestly seek God's will for his life. Bob felt God leading him to seminary, where he could finish his studies.

Bob's father did not celebrate his son's new life and told him flat out, "You're better off doing drugs than religion."

Bob's girlfriend came for a visit to St. Croix. We were all having dinner together one evening; she said that when he met her at the airport, all he could talk about was Jesus. She tried but couldn't get him to talk about anything other than Jesus. She said that they both had been baptized Catholic when they were infants, and that was enough.

Prayer is powerful. Bob, Clif, and I prayed for her

before she arrived on St. Croix. We prayed that God would save her. One evening after dinner, she and I spent some time together in the Bible. Some of her questions were cleared up, and God won the victory.

That night, she prayed and received Jesus as her Savior. After praying, she looked for Bob to tell him she had asked Jesus to save her. She found Bob kneeling in another room. He had been praying for her unceasingly about three hours while we were studying the Bible. She stayed with us for several weeks; it was a blessing to have her with us and to hear her witness to people as we passed out tracts on St. Croix.

The day arrived when we took Bob to the airport to board an airplane headed back for the States. We said goodbye to him with our blessings and with tears of joy. He left the island to return to his family and to attend seminary. Bob's life changed in exciting ways since he dared to say yes to God.

Isn't it amazing that God uses such unusual ways to answer prayers? We prayed that God would lead us to someone in need of Jesus. He used our longing to see Mark to give us a wishful thought, and then, with God's timing, we glimpsed Bob, who so resembled our son. The Lord knew that Bob was ready to hear the gospel. God also answered our prayers for his girlfriend to be saved.

God's amazing power changes lives and futures. God wants to change your life and future as you dare to say yes to God.

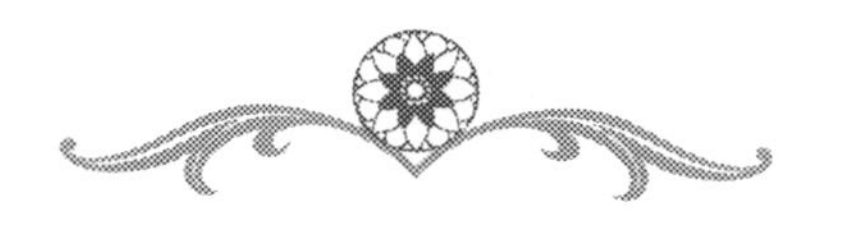

A Life Investment

As a son with the father, he hath
served with me in the Gospel.
—Philippians 2:22

In June 1971, the Harrigan family relocated from the British Island of Anguilla to St. Croix for economic reasons. They had four daughters and two sons. One son, Beltane, accepted Jesus as his personal Savior at the early age of eleven. He had grown in the Lord and had become very involved in his home church in Anguilla. He was sixteen when he was uprooted by the move.

Beltane became a member of the Sunny Isle Baptist Church, where Clif was pastor. He was a promising young boy with love and zeal for the Lord. He was elected as vice president of the youth group, which was growing in the Lord, and was involved in the life of the church. Beltane later shared that one of the highlights of his youth was the night a special program called "This Is Your Life" was presented, featuring him.

One day, Beltane and I were talking, and I mentioned, "God might call you to be a pastor or a missionary. Maybe you should think about going to Bible college."

However, Beltane had already made plans to go to an aviation school later in the summer, as he had always wanted to be a pilot. His brother was a commercial pilot, chartering people throughout the Caribbean islands. God wanted to be involved in Beltane's plans so that he would be the kind of pilot who would charter people to Jesus.

The summer of 1972 was a turning point in Beltane's life. He attended our Carib Camp, which we founded in the 1950s to minister Christ to young lives. Carib Camp was located in the Frederiksted rain forest on Creeky Dam Road, and God never had any trouble finding the address. We had such an exciting week with about twenty-five campers, some of whom had come to know Jesus as their Savior and some of whom had surrendered to live closer to the Lord.

At this camp session, Beltane shared, "The Lord has called me into the ministry to preach the gospel." His experience at Carib Camp had changed his life.

Later that summer, instead of attending aviation school, Beltane was accepted at the Blue Water Bible College on St. Thomas. He completed two years and then transferred to Tennessee Temple University, where he received a BA degree in Theology. While studying at Tennessee Temple, Beltane met Debbie Barnett, his future wife.

After graduating in 1979, he returned to St. Croix, proving himself in the ministry as he continued to work with the youth at the Sunny Isle Baptist Church. He also served as Clif's assistant pastor. But that's not all that happened to Beltane in 1979.

Wedding bells rang that same year, as Beltane and Debbie were joined together in matrimony. Clif performed the ceremony at Sunny Isle Baptist Church. God has blessed the Harrigans with two sons. The older son has answered God's call to be a missionary to the United States, and the younger son is being homeschooled.

Beltane is the founder and pastor of The Way of the Cross Baptist Church, established in 1982. The church has a strong emphasis on missions, since missionary efforts distinctly shaped Pastor Harrigan's life. He is also involved in evangelistic crusades throughout the Caribbean islands, the United States, and South America. His heart's cry and desire is to see souls saved. Beltane praises God for calling him into the ministry and allowing him to serve Him. We are so thankful that God gave us the opportunity to invest in Beltane's life and that God allowed Beltane to labor for the gospel alongside of us as a son in the Lord. God uses missionaries not only to present the gospel to the lost, but also to grow members of God's family so they can fulfill the assignments God has for them.

Daring to say yes, a young man invested his life and career in God's ministry. Praise the Lord for Beltane and his family. We love them.

Pastor Beltane Harrigan

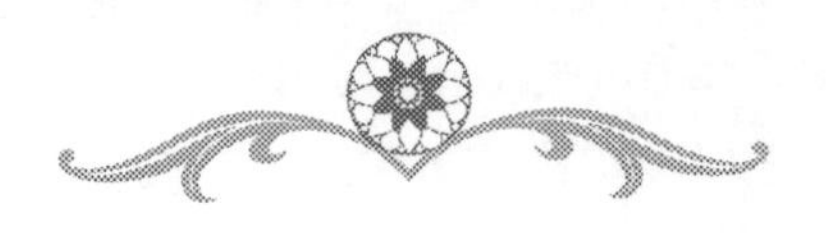

No Longer a Foster Child

For whoever shall do the will of God, he is
my brother and my sister and mother.
—Mark 3:35

Randy and his four brothers were natives of New York City, but their family originated from St. Croix. He and his brothers were sent back to St. Croix at a young age due to family circumstances. They were split up and put in various foster homes, with some scary and traumatic memories to show for it, including harsh beatings, running away, and sleeping in the streets.

However, one happy memory for the five little brothers was when they were taken to a revival meeting on St. Croix and for the first time heard about the love of God and about Jesus being crucified for their sins. That evening, they all made professions of faith in Jesus Christ as their personal Savior.

When Randy was ten years old, he had the privilege of living with some missionaries, Mr. and Mrs. Clyde Simpson, who ministered at the Altona Baptist Church. When the Simpsons went on furlough to the States, Randy was moved from foster home to foster home until he was finally settled into a foster home at Grove Place, towards the middle of the island. He told his new foster mother that he was of the Baptist faith and wanted to go to a Baptist church. He remembered meeting us through the Simpsons and began coming to our church in Frederiksted. A member of our church, Martha Raphael, invited him to attend Sunday school along with her own seven boys. Conrad Thomas was the dedicated bus driver, and he made it fun for all the kids to ride the bus to Sunday school.

Randy said, "I had some of the best times of my life learning the Bible in Sunday school. I remember one of the subjects that Sister Bubar taught: How to Defend Against False Doctrines and Cult Religions. I also remember hearing for the first time some messages on the pre-tribulation, mid-tribulation, and the millennium period that Pastor Bubar preached. One Sunday morning while Pastor Bubar was preaching, it was as if God spoke to me, saying, 'Randy, I want you to preach when you grow up.'"

Randy has other happy memories, including attending Carib Camp. He remembers playing softball on the side of the hill, and a funny incident where he was being initiated as an official Carib Camper. Randy was led, blindfolded, to kiss the Indian chief's ring (now don't laugh, but it was Clif, dressed like an Indian chief; camp isn't just for the kids). Randy kissed the ring, and his blindfold was removed; only then did Randy see the ring was on the Indian chief's big toe. Randy was grossed out and spitting and wiping his mouth until he saw the next new blindfolded camper kissing the chief's ring on the thumb and realized he had been tricked into thinking he kissed the toe; he really had kissed the ring on this thumb. There was lots of fun and laughter and crazy times for the campers.

Randy said, "Being at Carib Camp in an atmosphere of fun, Christian love, and fellowship, and learning the Bible, all helped to shape my life as a Christian. It all played an integral part in the spiritual development of my life."

When Randy returned from Carib Camp to his foster home, he wanted to continue to attend church and grow in knowledge and fellowship, but his foster mother would not allow him to attend regularly. This was a heartbreaking development; Randy felt so bad about it that he used to cry in bed at night. He was a twelve-year-old boy and needed the love, concern, and Bible teaching that he received from the church. Jesus said, "Let the children come to me, and forbid them not for such is the Kingdom of Heaven."

In the ninth grade, Randy learned to play the saxophone at school. He got great at it and was asked to be in steel drum band. The band pulled him away from the Lord, and by the age of sixteen, music had become such an important part of Randy's life that it was what he lived for.

After Randy graduated from high school in 1971, he attended the University of the Virgin Islands on St. Thomas to study law enforcement. He continued his college pursuit, switching back to the St. Croix campus and rejoining a steel drum band.

Randy also worked part-time at the Large Company; one day, he began talking about the Lord with a fellow worker. It turns out they had both been saved at a young age, but both had strayed away from the Lord. Randy mentioned that he knew us and suggested that they should try to get in touch with us. He and his friend actually left work to find us because they felt it was urgent for them to get back to the Lord. They stopped at a phone booth, looked up our number, and called us, but there was no answer. Just then, to their surprise, they saw us passing by in our car.

Randy hung up the phone and tried to flag us down, but a tractor trailer came between us, and we didn't see him. Later that night, Randy called us and made an appointment for him and his friend to come and talk with Clif. Randy kept the appointment, but his friend did not. Clif shared the Scriptures with Randy and prayed with him. Later, Randy prayed and made things right with the Lord; he said that it felt like a huge weight was lifted off of him and he felt so happy in the Lord. He told his foster mother about his decision for Jesus, and he also declared that he was going to quit the band and start living for the Lord.

When Randy told the band members about his decision to quit, they were perplexed and asked, "How could you get saved in one night?"

Randy told them, "That's the way it happens."

The band members didn't believe him because he wasn't even going to church, worshipping, or serving the Lord. Just like Nicodemus said to Jesus as he was trying to figure out salvation intellectually, the band members asked Randy, "How could that be?"

Randy told them that he was saved when he was a little boy, and he was giving his life back to the Lord.

The band members said, "In three weeks, you'll be back with us." They were wrong; it has been thirty years, and Randy has not gone back to that kind of life. Praise God.

When Randy surrendered his life to the Lord, he also

surrendered his musical talent. He began playing the steel drums and is well known for his music. He was invited to give concerts at the First Baptist Church in Atlanta, where Reverend Charles Stanley is pastor. Randy has also produced several music CDs and composed music, but his favorites are still the old-time hymns and gospel music.

After Randy repented and returned with all his heart to the Lord, he attended Sunny Isle Baptist Church faithfully, just like he had wanted to do as a child but was prohibited from doing. He also remembered that God called him to preach when he was a child. Randy entered the Blue Water Bible College on St. Thomas in 1973 and attended until 1975. He also helped Clif with the youth at Sunny Isle Baptist Church. He then continued his studies at Tennessee Temple in Chattanooga, where he earned a BA degree in Bible and did some work on his master's in religious education.

After graduating from Tennessee Temple in 1978, Randy started the New Life Baptist Church, where he pastored until 1987. He then started the Roanoke Community Church and was pastor for eleven years. In 1997, he was called to pastor the Mt. Paran Missionary Baptist Church in Chattanooga.

The Lord has really blessed his ministry, and on May 21, 2006, the church celebrated Randy's ninth year as their pastor. We were invited to attend, and Clif was the guest speaker for the anniversary service. It was a blessing to feel the sweet spirit in the church and to witness the congregation's love for the Lord and for Pastor Randy, his wife Magella, and their fine sons.

Much prayer and labor made it a special event and a great time of fellowship. The choir and musicians presented absolutely awesome selections. Following the service, there was a wonderful dinner prepared by members of the church. This was really a nostalgic time for us, as it reminded us of the great times of fellowship we had in the churches on St. Croix.

While we worshipped at Randy and Magella's lovely home, we were also rewarded with getting acquainted with two of Pastor Randy's brothers (now grown men), who were present for the celebration. They are both wonderful Christian men. In fact, one of them teaches the adult Sunday school class we attended at Mt. Paran, and his wife is from one of our churches on St. Croix. She also taught a Sunday school class. It was truly a heart-warming experience to reminisce with the three brothers about their youth on St. Croix.

God's love and mercy guided the five little brothers through trying childhood days and into manhood and into servanthood. We thank God that He used us as missionaries to encourage Randy to follow God's call to preach. God's infinite love and mercy never gave up on Randy but tugged and burned within his heart to bring him back into fellowship with God. To God be the glory.

Upon our arrival home in Florida after the anniversary service, we received a gift of money for a cruise. It was Randy's way of showing his appreciation to us for the love and interest we had taken in him as a young boy on St. Croix Island.

Randy dared to say yes to God and to leave the life he knew for something bigger, God's vision for his life. He now has taken his rightful place in the family of God, no longer a foster child but a child of the King – with many brothers and sisters, fathers and mothers who are doing the will of God. God is so good.

A New Husband

Rejoicing in hope; patient in tribulation;
continuing instant in prayers.
—Romans 12:12

We lived in a multicultural neighborhood on St. Croix, where there were Crucians, Arabs, Spaniards, and Indians, along with a Mainiac (Clif) and a Michagander (me) to round out the diversity. One of the pleasures of this was all the different cuisines. We were introduced to Indian food, called *roti* by our neighbors. Flour was kneaded, rolled thin, and fried on both sides. Then curried goat, beef, or chicken was spooned onto a flat roti pancake and folded like a diaper. We held it with both hands in order to eat it. Mmm, mmm, good! Clif liked the beef roti, and my favorite was chicken. Our Crucian-born son liked goat roti and still does. Is there anyone who doesn't like roti? We love roti.

Mark made friends with the neighbor children, and some of them came to church with us. They learned about Jesus in Sunday school and prayed to receive Jesus as their Savior. One Sunday evening, we were showing a Billy Graham film at the church. The children asked their mother if she would come to see the film with them; she initially declined, until her daughter begged her to come, and she changed her mind.

We were praying for the family. Imagine the joy we felt that Sunday when the mother and her four children climbed into our vehicle to go to church. They met some wonderful Christian people at the Sunny Isle Baptist Church. They welcomed her and showed her Christian love and fellowship.

When she saw the film and heard Billy Graham preach the gospel, it stirred her heart. After the film, Clif gave an invitation for those who wanted to know more about Jesus and be saved. She went forward to hear more about Jesus. Sister Marks, a faithful prayer warrior in the church, ministered to her. That night, she prayed to receive Jesus as her Savior and was wonderfully saved. She also later was baptized by Clif. When a newborn baby is born, you're not sure what they're going to be yet. It was the same with this newborn babe in Christ. We had no idea that she was going to have a faith that just wouldn't quit; no matter how long it took, she would just keep marching forward like the Energizer Bunny.

She had been brought up in the Hindu religion. When she was a child, she practiced Hinduism. It was the religion of her parents, her grandparents, and her ancestors. The burning of candles, praying for the dead, and worshipping idols in their home were all rituals of Hinduism, their Indian heritage. She was taught that Hindus had the freedom to choose to work toward spiritual perfection by pulling themselves up by doing good works.

Hinduism has an explanation for the suffering anyone experiences, whether sickness, starvation, or disaster. It is attributed to the evil actions that the person suffering must surely have done in a previous life. She believed that the soul will one day be free of the cycle of rebirths.

Her childhood left her with memories of fear and darkness after the death of her loved ones. She stood by at the funerals of her grandmother, her grandfather, and her father, watching fire consume their bodies with no future hope.

During the Billy Graham film, she heard of hope. It was explained in a simple and plain way. The blood of Jesus shed on the cross was payment for our sins. Jesus made it possible for us to have hope beyond the grave. We just need to ask Him to save us. "Not by the works of righteousness which we have done, but according to his mercy He saved us" (Titus 3:5).

If only her grandparents and parents had been reached by the gospel, their departure would have been a joyous one, with a future hope of heaven. They could have said as Paul said, "Absent from the body means to be present with the Lord" (2 Corinthians 5:8).

She and her children continued to come to Sunny Isle Baptist Church. She was eager to learn more about Jesus. She went with the visitation group, going door to door, witnessing and sharing Christ. She earnestly prayed for those in her family who were Hindu. Her mother and some of her sisters and two brothers have become Christians in answer to her faithful intercession.

She also wanted her husband to be saved and prayed every day that he would turn to the Lord and be saved. He came to church with her sometimes and seemed to have a desire for the Lord at that time, but he was under the control of alcohol and did not respond to the call of salvation.

Around two o'clock one night, we were aroused from sleep by the sound of iron striking metal and shattering glass. We knew something terrifying was happening. Then we heard a rap on our door. It was the mother and her four children. They had snuck out of their house to come to our house for safety. She and the children were visibly shaken.

She said, "My husband has a terrible drinking problem, and he does very obnoxious things when he drinks. He's been drinking all day and into the night, and when he got home from the bar, he got out of his truck and told the truck lights to go out. When they didn't go out, he beat on them with a piece of iron, smashing the lights on our new truck. Then he came into the house and pulled a light fixture out of the ceiling and wall. I was afraid of fire as sparks were flying everywhere. As I went through the door, he threw a heavy pair of tin snips that embedded in the door. He was in a state of drunken fury. I pray every day that God will save my husband and change his life and that we can have peace in our home." Who knows what we would be like if not saved?

She and her children continued to come to church, where she found comfort in the Bible; she found a phrase that really stood out to her: "And it came to pass." She quoted it in her gentle manner as God brought her through each trial and heartache. Our hearts were crushed for her as we saw episodes caused by alcohol. We thought she did extremely well under such dreadful circumstances. Her motto became, "As for me and my children, we will serve the Lord."

It takes a lot of faith and determination to stand by a mate who is so inhumane at times. Yet her heart still communicated love and compassion toward him, and she never ceased praying for him. She's not only a hearer of God's Word, she is also a doer. She practices what she learns.

We marvel at the grace and peace that God has given her to cope with grim circumstances. Some of the moments in her life have been frantic, but with new life in Christ and a hope for the future, her confidence is in the Lord, and her faith in Him has never wavered. She always spoke with such wisdom and common sense.

Sometimes, she would say, "I wonder what Jesus would do?"

She and her family are precious jewels for whom Christ died.

She and her husband moved to Florida, and in 2006, we were overjoyed to attend her seventieth birthday celebration. Some of her family and friends came from St. Croix. We all rejoiced. The dinner at her daughter and son-in-law's lovely home was typical delicious West Indian fare. A joyous time.

She has been on mission trips with her church, distributing hundreds of Bibles and thousands of tracts to people in the Bahamas and Mexico. She still prays for her husband without wavering.

She said, "I used to beg him to come to church with me. Now I let the Lord speak to him, and he goes with me."

She has been praying faithfully for him for many years.

Guess what? In 2009, she called me to share that her husband finally made a decision for Jesus Christ and was going to be baptized. She saw the fruits of her labor and steadfastness. Because her faith just wouldn't quit, her husband finally had to quit his old life instead. This is a woman whose faith and determination just wouldn't quit, no matter what. To God be the glory.

Dare to say yes to God.

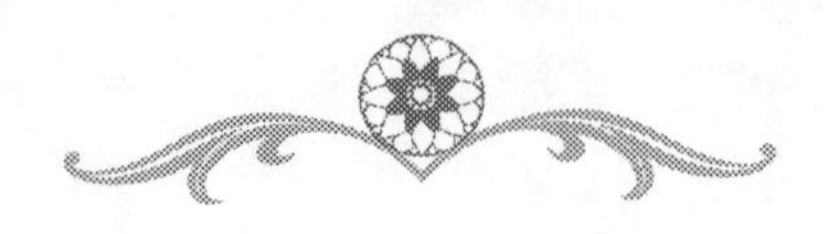

From Saigon to St. Croix

Now therefor ye are no more strangers
and foreigners, but fellow citizens with the
saints and of the house hold of God.
—Ephesians 2:19

Hai grew up in a traditional Vietnamese family in Tan An, about fifty-five miles southwest of Saigon. Hai and her seven brothers and sisters were raised in the Buddhist religion. Her father was killed in a truck accident when she was about eighteen. She moved to Saigon, and her mother died of a mysterious illness about a year later. From 1968 to 1972, she worked at whatever job she could find to support her family; whether it was selling lottery tickets, weaving baskets, or factory work, sometimes her workday was from five in the morning until midnight.

Like other Buddhists, Hai believed in God and in the laws that teach obedience, faithfulness, and love. She burned joss sticks and paper money and made the traditional offerings of rice and fruit to appease the spirits. Hai was very faithful to these practices until late in 1970, when she met her husband, Lewis. Lewis was an American air traffic controller stationed in Saigon for two years.

Hai took a vow to spend the rest of her life with Lewis.

This meant leaving her family and country behind. It was a desperate time in Vietnam then, and the US military was about to pull out. Hai didn't want to leave her family, but she couldn't let her husband go back to the United States alone. She felt sad, but she had to choose the best way to make everyone else's lives better in the long run.

Hai and Lewis were married in Honolulu and then moved to New Hampshire. Spiritually, Hai had no place to turn and no way to talk to God. The joss sticks she burned on the fireplace mantle looked so out of place. Hai had left her God in Vietnam and felt very alone, afraid, and unprotected. This tempered her sense of boundless freedom.

Hai's mother-in-law knew she had a thirst to know God, so she gave her a Vietnamese Bible translation and introduced her to Bible studies at her church. Hai struggled with feelings of guilt and betrayal over leaving behind the religion of her family. The emotions were very painful. She felt that cutting herself off from Buddhism was putting everything that had been meaningful in her life, including her family, behind her, but she continued in her study. It was all she had.

In time, Lewis accepted a job in Taipei, Taiwan. There she joined a Navy Christian women's club; she attended their Bible studies and read books to learn about Jesus Christ. In Buddhism, she understood how to worship, but now she understood who to worship and why, as well.

One rainy day at a Navy chapel on the outskirts of Taipei, a guest speaker talked about Christ's sacrifice. Hai found what she had been looking for and sensed that she couldn't delay anymore. The speaker's message took away her guilt that her mother would think she had betrayed the family and the Buddhist religion.

That day, Hai accepted Jesus into her life. He took away her sins and her fears. She was no longer separated from God. She had someone to pray to, and many of her prayers have been answered. From that day, Hai continued to grow closer to Jesus.

The Navy worship services were broadcast over the air; many of her Chinese and American friends learned of her decision and rejoiced with her. Lewis was pleasantly surprised, and he, too, accepted Jesus as his Lord and Savior.

After a trail of stepping-stones, Lewis took a job in Puerto Rico as an air traffic controller and then retired on St. Croix, where he built a beautiful house on a hill overlooking the Caribbean. Hai and Lewis attended a church across town until they met us. They attended the Easter sunrise service at Southgate Baptist Church and got involved in church activities. They became our good friends, and through Bible studies, they were inspired to take their faith more seriously. On June 23, 1991, Clif baptized both Lewis and Hai in the Caribbean Sea. They became members of the Southgate Baptist Church.

Lewis became a deacon and worked with the trustees on construction projects. The church was growing. An additional Sunday school building was needed. Lewis gave skilled help, along with other men from Southgate. Beautiful Sunday school classrooms were constructed on property extending from the church. Hai was a deaconess and enjoyed being coordinator for both the kitchen and social hours after church.

Back to Vietnam: Hai and Lewis returned to visit Hai's

family in Vietnam. They flew to Bangkok, Thailand, and then onto Saigon. Brothers and sisters, and nieces and nephews, met them at the airport. Hai was so happy to see them after twenty-two years. Finally, they were reunited.

Hai said, "I visited my brothers and sisters, and the Lord answered my prayer that He would lead me to tell my family about Jesus. My sister, Chieu, who was also a Buddhist, had married a Catholic. She talked about praying to Mary instead of Jesus, so I handed her the Vietnamese Bible that my mother-in-law had given me twenty-years earlier. She went home and read it and said she could not find anything in it about praying to Mary.

"I hope that she can study that book [the Bible] and get to know Christ better," she continued. "Maybe God can help others come to know Him. I am praying that my family will learn about Christ through other Christians.

"We returned to St. Croix from Vietnam on March 31, 1994. God led and protected us on the whole trip, answering all our prayers. Once again, He has led me safely from Saigon to St. Croix, US Virgin Island."

Clif and I are thrilled that God opened the door for Hai and Lewis to go back to South Vietnam to help build a church. It's been exciting to receive email updates on the building progress. They've been faithful in keeping us posted, even when they were detoured to a hospital for tests, due to several sick days.

We wish we were there to help them. It brings back good memories when we were missionaries building churches on St. Croix. We're praying for them as they serve the Lord and pray that all of Hai's family will be saved.

Here's an excerpt from an email Lewis sent us from Vietnam:

"This construction team of ours is so highly skilled and versatile, I've yet to see a task they cannot do and do well! In the beginning, there was a lot of shoveling to do and they really put their backs into it. Then there was steel to cut and bend, forms to build, concrete to mix, pour and float and a roof to build."

Lewis and his team of workers are planting a church that will leave a beautiful legacy behind, pointing people to Jesus Christ, the Savior of the world. What a legacy.

Hai and Lewis said, "Yes, God, we will go help build a church in Saigon, Vietnam."

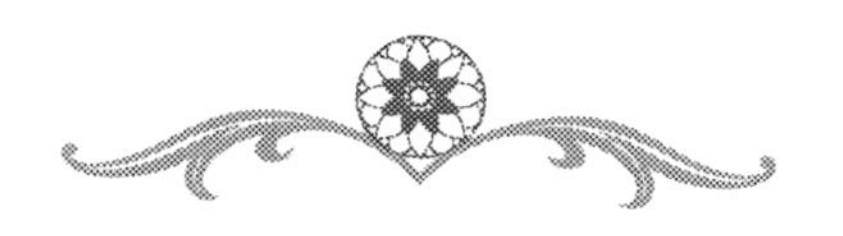

The Walking Bible

Thy word have I hid in mine heart, that
I might not sin against thee.

—Psalm 119:11

Have you ever tried to remember something but couldn't? I have a hard time remembering names. How do we learn? We learn by hearing when we are children, long before we learn to read. Hearing, repeating, and writing things down all help us not only learn but remember.

We were given a beautiful green Amazon parrot from the tropical island of Trinidad. We named him Trinita. Each morning, I would say to him, "Good morning."

Finally, one morning, the parrot surprised us when he said, "Good morning." He imitated what I had said to him over and over. Even though Trinita didn't understand my language, he learned the words that I repeated: "Good morning."

Since we learn by hearing, repeating, and memorizing, our family decided to memorize some of the Bible. Mark was nine years old at the time. Together we memorized Romans chapter 10, all twenty-one verses. We recited the chapter at Sunny Isle Baptist Church where we pastored. The blessing of hiding God's Word in our hearts to share with others far outweighed the actual challenge of memorizing it.

Our decision to memorize Bible verses inspired others to take up the challenge, as well. Teenagers and adults in the church learned whole chapters of the Bible. During the Sunday evening services, Clif would give individuals the opportunity to recite a chapter in between songs. As a chapter was quoted, verse by verse from memory, the congregation followed along in their Bibles. It was an exciting time in our church. Many were hiding the Word of God in their hearts.

A particularly outstanding example was Mrs. Richards, who began memorizing the Bible when she was in her fifties. She learned a new chapter almost every week. She memorized nine complete books of the New Testament, plus four whole chapters from the Gospel of Matthew and four from the book of John. Mrs. Richards soon earned the name "the Walking Bible." If you are going to be called a name, this is a great one to be called. Wherever Mrs. Richards went, those Bible chapters were carried in her heart and mind.

Mr. and Mrs. Richards were faithful to the Lord and to the church. They went on visitation with a group from church every Tuesday evening and each Sunday afternoon. Mr. Richards could quote scriptures and find verses in the Bible easily as he shared Jesus with others. Mr. Richards served as an usher at church and drove the church bus.

The last time I spoke with Mrs. Richards, she said her husband had passed away due to diabetes. At that time, she was sixty-seven years old and said, "I am still memorizing scriptures, but the older I get, the longer it takes to learn a chapter. But I'm still working at it."

The love of God's Word has strengthened her and her testimony, and she has grown to love the Lord the more she spends time in His Word.

Wouldn't you like to be called a special name, like "the Walking Bible"? You can, you know. If you memorize one verse a week, you will know fifty-two verses in one year. What a blessing.

Let's be like Mrs. Richard and say yes to God.

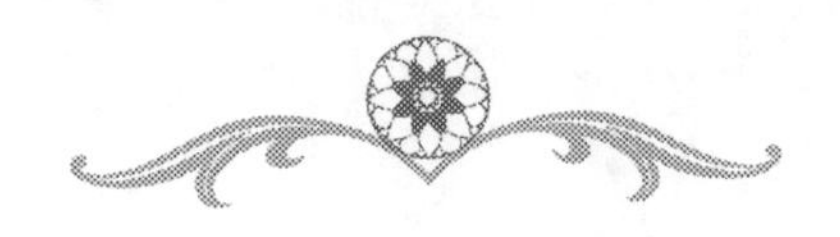

Gift from God

And we know that all things work together
for good to them that love God, to them who
are called according to His purpose.
—Romans 8:28

Clif and I became friends with a couple we led in a Bible study in their home. They were a delightful couple with three children. Sarah was of Spanish descent, born in Puerto Rico, and Sonny was a Crucian, born on the island of St. Croix. They were expecting another child. One day, the call came: "It's a girl." Clif and I hurried to our car and drove to the hospital in Christiansted.

Sonny met us, walking down the corridor of the hospital. His facial expression betrayed his usual cheerful look. He said, "The doctor thinks that the baby's life expectancy will be only a few years, twelve at the most."

The doctor had said that baby Lilly may have Down syndrome, which was later confirmed.

At times like this, what does a pastor say to a mother and father of a new born infant with the possibility of Down syndrome? And what could he say to undo the fears left by their former priest, who told them, "It's God's punishment, because you left the Catholic church and turned to the Baptist religion"?

We talked with Sarah and Sonny, and assured them that God is infallible, loving, and merciful. He chose their special Christian home for the baby Lilly. God entrusted this precious little one to their care, knowing that with Sarah and Sonny's love for Jesus, she would be safe and secure in their home.

God's guiding hand had prepared them for their future, which would include baby Lilly. Sarah had found encouragement and strength through Bible studies with me. We prayed together for the salvation of her husband, and Sonny became saved while studying the Bible with Clif. Sarah and Sonny's love and faith in Jesus Christ proved to be more than just religion, as they because faithful, loving servants of the Lord. Sonny was a deacon and teacher, and Sarah played the organ and taught a class. Their older daughters attended Christian colleges. One attended Bethel College in St. Paul, Minnesota, and the other attended Liberty University in Lynchburg, Virginia. Their son worked Stateside.

Lilly's parents bought her a beautiful piano, and Kathy, a Christian lady taught her to read music. She diligently practiced and learned to play the piano, using her talent for the Lord. She played the opening worship hymn in the services at the Southgate Baptist Church every Sunday morning. Lilly invited Jesus to be her Savior, and she is now a prayer pillar in the church and never misses a prayer meeting. Lilly was always the alarm clock for their household to be at services.

Lilly wasn't expected to live beyond twelve years of age, but on September 2, 2014, she became a walking miracle, still alive at age fifty. She is in good health and is the queen of their home, having captured the love, attention, and understanding of everyone. Lilly's life shows that God has a plan for everyone who submits to His love and will. How wonderful that we are each created with our own talents and limitations, but we all have a place in God's kingdom and ways to bring Him glory. God's gift of life is far too precious to eliminate before birth.

I ran across a letter that Sarah had written us some years ago. When Lilly was seven years old, she suffered from a serious diverticulitis problem. She required an operation and was bed-ridden in the hospital for about a month; she had to learn to walk again. Her mother stated in her letter, "Our spiritual life was strong; the Lord provided two friends and spiritual guides, Pastor and Mrs. Bubar. They helped us all the way from the beginning. May God bless them always. As a mother, I do not know how I could have made it through without the Lord and the faithful missionaries that God gave us."

Lilly's mother, Sarah Johansen, went home to be with the Lord on October 13, 2008. Lilly is still strong and doing well. She still has her father, Sonny Johansen, two sisters, Sally and Sandy, and a brother, Tommy. They all know the Lord as their Savior, including Lilly. It's amazing to hear Lilly pray. She often prayed at our church, and her prayers moved our hearts and surely moved God's, as well.

Kathy was Lilly's piano teacher. She said, "Teaching piano and loving Lilly has been among the most rewarding experiences of my life. I could never have imagined the friendship I would have missed had I silenced that still small voice … and Lilly's serious plea for piano lessons. She had been praying for several years for a teacher so she could play like her much-loved mother."

"I would have missed the joy of helping a friend of Jesus transform into a 24/7 worshipper and pure-hearted young woman of thirty-four going on eight. The life-changing difference this small time spent on Lilly's music lessons brought more of a gift to me than to Lilly – the best of a true Christian life-long friend."

Kathy dared to say, "Yes, God, I will teach Lilly to play the piano. I will serve You." What a blessing.

Sonny and three children: Sandy, Sally, and Lilly

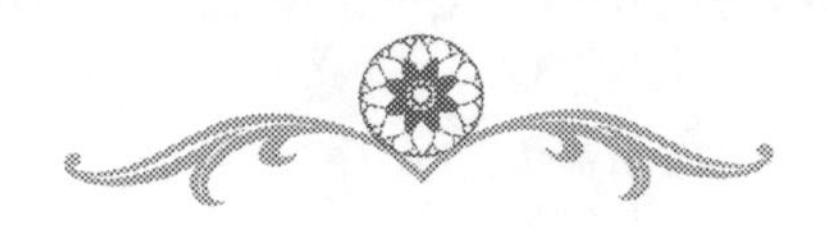

Think Big; We've Got a Big God

Now unto him that is able to do exceedingly
abundantly above all that we ask or think,
according to the power that worketh in us, unto
Him be glory in the Church by Christ Jesus
throughout all ages, world without end. Amen.
—Ephesians 3:20–21

Clif bought an accordion for me after we knew we were going to be missionaries in St. Croix. It helped with music in the open-air meetings and with the children's Bible clubs at the Carib Youth Camp. They loved to sing with the accordion. We lived in Frederiksted near a small music store. One day, I moseyed into the store and spied a laptop chord organ; I reasoned that if I had a chord organ, I could learn to play it for church services. It cost $75, which was a lot; I knew we couldn't afford a larger one. Our monthly support was only $200.

The store owner said he was willing to take $10 down and that I could pay $10 a month until it was paid for. That seemed doable, but I told him that I would have to check with my husband first and then come back.

The store owner was a smart salesman and said, "Just take it home with you; no problem."

The man was so willing for me to have the little chord organ that he signed me up immediately. I was delighted that he was so willing to work with me; I knew it just must be the Lord. I signed the contract and couldn't wait to get home to show my laptop chord organ to Clif and explain the low payment contract.

When Clif saw it, he said, "Where did you get that toy?" and told me to take it back.

I was very embarrassed but had to return to the store and return the organ; the storeowner was very nice about it, however. Little did I know that God had something bigger in mind for me.

Several months passed, and it was now May 2, my birthday. Clif gave me a birthday card, and as I opened it, a picture of a new organ fell out. Clif had ordered me one from Miami. The day the huge carton arrived by truck, I was so excited and thrilled. Have you ever received something so wonderful that you really wanted but couldn't afford? That's God. He knows the desires of your heart. The organ was a beautiful electric Hammond organ, a floor model. We both were so happy that the Lord had made it possible. Clif always has felt that if anything is worth doing, it's worth doing well. That was his attitude about what organ I should have and also his attitude when building churches. He always searched for good materials, the best prices, and attractive church designs. He built the churches well, strong, and beautiful.

With prayer and God's help, I learned to play the Hammond organ in our home. When we finished building the Frederiksted Baptist Church, we moved the

Hammond organ there so I could play it for services. After some time, the church was able to purchase its own organ, so we moved the Hammond organ to the Sunny Isle Baptist Church, where I played it until they could purchase an organ. Then we moved it to the third church we built, Southgate Baptist Church. You guessed it: They were eventually able to purchase an organ. The Lord provided an organ that blessed all three churches until they could afford their own. At each church, I was happy to share my Hammond organ and play it at the services.

After thirty-six years of missionary service on St. Croix, we sensed that our mission was accomplished. We gave the Hammond organ to Conrad Thomas. He had been a member of our Frederiksted Baptist Church. Conrad studied a Bible course from Liberty University and in later years purchased a former Kingdom Hall building in New Town and converted it to a Baptist church. We moved the Hammond organ to that church, and Conrad Thomas became pastor, bus driver, and organist. As far as we know, the Hammond organ is still going strong for the Lord on St. Croix. It was a blessing in four churches, as it ended up in Conrad's church.

It was a hard day when I had to return the little laptop chord organ. But I'm reminded of what Corrie Ten Boom once said: "Obedience is easy when you know a God who never makes mistakes in guiding you." I didn't know that God had bigger plans. He delights in doing exceedingly abundantly above all that we ask or think. That's our God.

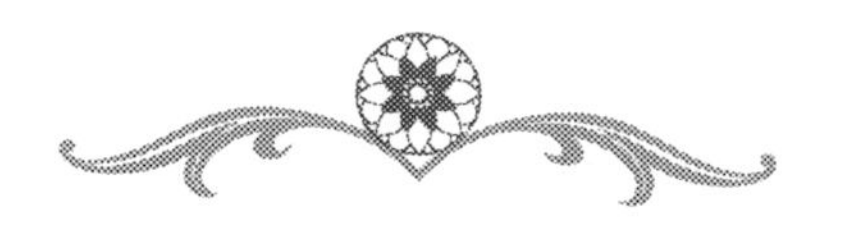

A Boyhood Dream: Flying

Delight yourself also in the Lord and he shall give thee the desires of thine heart.

—Psalm 37:4

Like many little boys, Clif dreamed of one day flying an airplane. In his classrooms in Maine, Clif expressed his dream by carefully folding his spelling papers into the shapes of airplanes and cleared them for take-off when the teachers weren't looking. Other boys caught the vision and began to fold their own airplanes and test them in flight.

From such humble beginnings, God watched over Clif's dream and made it come true through a sequence of events over the years. It really compels us to think how God led us step-by-step to the fulfillment of that dream for His glory and our joy. As we dared to say yes to God, He said yes to us with many blessings throughout the years. He made sure we were in the right place at the right time for this dream to come to pass. The Bible says in Psalm 37:23, "The steps of a good man are ordered by the Lord."

Because we dared to say yes to God's call on our lives, He could position us in St. Croix and then, in 1955, moved a Christian family, the McCrearys, next door to us. They became members of the Frederiksted Baptist Church.

Interesting thing about Gordon McCreary: He just happened to be an owner of a little one-engine Luscombe airplane. He flew the plane from New York to St. Croix, and that was an exciting adventure in that little two-seater airplane. Gordon was a clever pilot and had thought to strap an extra gas tank inside the plane on the floor next to the seat with a hose and hand pump, to pump gas into the plane's tank should it run out of gas.

Gordon enjoyed flying and enjoyed sharing the experience with Clif. He would ask Clif to go flying with him, and Gordon would hand-crank the prop while Clif would trig the wheel and pull the propeller, then both would jump into the plane and take off down the runaway at Alexandria Hamilton Airport. Once in the air, Gordon would show Clif how to fly and operate the plane.

One day, he said, "Clif, use the plane to take some lessons and get your pilot's license."

Some of Clif's flight lessons were unforgettable. I remember one day in particular when I was visiting Carmen Navarro, the Spanish pastor's wife. We were busy chatting when we heard an airplane approaching. We looked up and identified the shiny spot in the sky as a Luscombe airplane. We watched as the plane proceeded to spiral down ever closer to the earth. This caused us to pray fervently; finally, the plane leveled off, and disaster was averted. I learned later what happened. Gordon was teaching Clif what to do in case the airplane went into a nosedive or tailspin, and Clif was practicing his response.

Clif continued to take flight lessons and finally obtained his own pilot's license.

Now God knew that Clif would want something more than a paper airplane to fly at this time in his life, so sometime later, it turned out that Ludvig Johansen, another member of our church, bought a Cessna 172 for his son, who was a pilot and mechanic. Ludi knew that Clif had a license to fly, so whenever we planned to take a vacation, Ludi told Clif to take the plane. God is so good.

The first time we flew it, Ludi said to me before we left, "Pastor Bubar is crazy, but you are even crazier because you are going to climb into that little airplane and fly with him."

He had a sense of humor, and we both chuckled, but his remark got me thinking, and soon I was taking flying lessons too. I reasoned that in case Clif fell asleep, I would know how to fly the plane.

When Ludi learned of my reasoning, he said, "If Pastor Bubar falls asleep, you just need to wake him up."

I explained that I was talking about another sleep, but even if the plane went down, we would simply go up. One of the bonuses of being a Christian is God's promise of a home beyond the grave. A Christian's destination is heaven, and this flight plan holds true to course, regardless of whether we exit this life due to an airplane crash or natural causes.

One day when Clif was at the airport, he spotted a red and white Cessna 182; he was able to look past its flat tires and dusty panels to see its potential, the wonderful purpose it was created for. Clif found that the owner of the plane had abandoned it to decay, having left the island and the loan he owed on the plane. Clif went to the bank and made an offer on the plane, but the bank refused it. We were disappointed but God wasn't. God had a plan.

Several weeks later, the bank called and said they had reconsidered Clif's offer, and if he was still willing to pay the price, the plane would become his. Clif went over to the airport to cast a longing glance at the airplane, only to be told that it had been sold. Clif's heart skipped a beat. He asked who bought it, and the man replied that a man from Maine had bought it.

Clif breathed a sigh of relief and said, "That's me."

The plane flourished in Clif's care and took to the skies again.

Clif and I have witnessed God's tender loving care in providing not only for our needs but many times for our wants, as well. He has given us the desire of our hearts, just like He promised those who love and serve Him.

Several years later, we flew from St. Croix to the States on furlough. We attended a Baptist General Missionary conference and then flew to Maine to visit Clif's parents. On our way to Maine, we stopped to gas up at a small airport in Massachusetts. The young man refueling the plane was a pilot and flight instructor.

He said to us, "I sure like your airplane. I'd like to buy it."

Clif asked him, "How much do you like it?" He pointed to a like-new demonstrator plane and joked, "I'll trade you for that one."

After the young man finished fueling our plane, we talked. When he found out we were headed for Maine, he remarked that his parents went to Maine every summer, where they rented a cottage on a lake. It just so happened that we were constructing a cottage on a lake in Maine, where Clif's father cut trees and sawed them into lumber that we used to build the cottage when we came home on furlough.

When the young pilot heard this, he arranged to bring his parents to see the cottage and perhaps make a deal with us. Clif's father was not wild about the idea of his family flying over water in a twenty-year-old plane with few instruments, so he sweetened the deal by offering to throw in a piece of land on the lake if that would clinch the deal.

As it turned out, we exchanged our cottage, the piece of land on the lake, and the old Cessna for the like-new Cessna 182, and the papers were signed swiftly with no money involved. God works in wondrous ways. The young pilot was happy with our old Cessna, and our like-new Cessna soon became spiritually employed. Clif's flying dream had finally come true. God gave more abundantly than we ever dreamed of. Our Cessna 182 airplane was a blessing to us and to others for many years. It was all part of God's plan.

The airplane that God blessed us with served faithfully as a carrier of Bibles and Christian literature and books that were distributed by the Choice Book ladies to other islands throughout the Caribbean. Our plane also served the Lord by carrying sick people from St. Croix to Puerto Rico, where they could obtain the special medical attention that they needed. It flew back and forth to Puerto Rico as Clif bought necessary materials in San Juan. It carried gallons of paint and other materials to missionaries who were building churches on other islands. It flew clothes and food to the island of Dominica after a devastating hurricane. It also carried us from St. Croix to the States and back on furlough.

Our son, Mark, Toady (our little poodle), and I all felt at ease flying a long journey over water with just one engine, as long as Missionary Pilot Clifford Bubar was at the control. We didn't even worry when we flew over the Bermuda Triangle, while Mark simultaneously read excerpts from a book about mysterious disappearances of planes in that area.

We are so thankful to God for his protection as we flew over many miles of water, land, and sea in our little one-engine airplane. We also thank the Lord for giving us the common sense to be fair weather flyers, not putting ourselves or others in jeopardy by starting off in bad weather during any of those twenty-five years of safe flying. Clif probably learned to be cautious at an early age when gauging conditions suitable for flying airplanes safely and undetected past the teachers.

God gave Clif a dream in childhood and was faithful to bring it to completion.

Clif and LeEllen

Gunshot Tragedy

Cast thy bread upon the waters: for thou
shalt find it after many days.
—Ecclesiastes 11:1

One day, I received a telephone call when we were living in town. The caller described a tragedy that had happened a few days earlier. Two teenage friends were playing with a gun. One of the boys pointed the gun at his friend and said, "I'm going to shoot." His friend said, "Shoot." The boy pulled the trigger, and the gun blasted with a loud noise. The boy who was shot was rushed to the hospital. The doctor found that the bullet was lodged in the boy's head in a very critical place that didn't allow for its removal. Neither boy had realized that the gun was actually loaded. No one should ever point a gun at anyone, even when playing.

The boy had to lie perfectly flat and still on his back at the hospital. The caller said that the boy's mouth was very dry and parched, but he couldn't drink water. The doctor said that he could be allowed some pieces of ice if someone would put it in his mouth.

The boy's parents were becoming extremely exhausted from caring for him day and night at the hospital, and the caller asked if we could help. We expressed our sympathy and said that we would be glad to help. Clif stayed one night, and I stayed the next night, rotating that way for a couple of weeks. We stayed by his bedside, feeding him ice as he required it in place of water.

It was a wonderful opportunity to share Christian love and to witness for Jesus. One never knows what the seed planted might bring forth later. Ecclesiastes 11:1 says, "Cast your bread upon the waters, for after many days you will find it again." God often turned tragedies into opportunities for us to show people that we genuinely cared for them, and we could earn the right to share our faith in Jesus Christ.

When the boy was released to go home to recuperate, his uncle presented us with money, but we would not accept it. We told him that we appreciated it, but we were glad to help and were thankful to our awesome God that he had spared the boy's life.

Later, when we purchased some property in the town of Frederiksted to build a church, we needed a surveyor. An acquaintance said, "Do you remember the two boys who were fooling around with a gun and one boy shot the other boy? The boy that was shot was my nephew. I remember that you two both stayed with him in the hospital. I appreciate your kindness and the interest that you showed toward my nephew and the family. I am going to survey the church property at no charge for you."

Time and time again, we have seen the providence of God taking care of our needs, as we cared for the needs of others. Our God is an awesome God, and He reigns from heaven above.

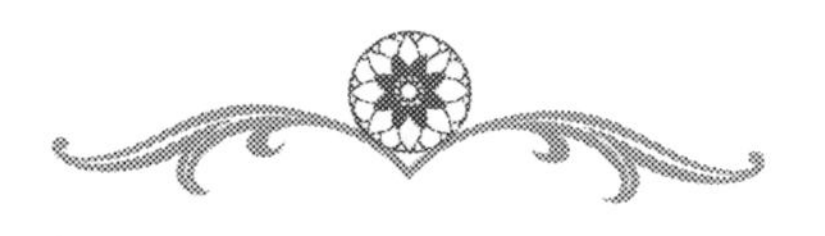

Bittersweet

For I am persuaded, that neither death, nor life, nor angels, nor principalities, nor powers, nor things present, nor things to come, Nor height, nor depth, nor any other creature, shall be able to separate us from the love of God which is in Christ Jesus our Lord.

—Romans 8:38

I need to tell this story because it points out how intimately God carries us through bittersweet tragedies. Excerpts are taken from some of the letters we received from our friend's son while he was in prison, waiting to be executed.

We became friendly with a couple at their workplace. They were lovely people, a little younger than us. They were from South America but had been longtime residents of St. Croix. Their religious background was Catholic, and in addition, they had read books about other religions and philosophies and had a hard time accepting that salvation comes by faith in Jesus and not by works. Still, they invited us to their home to have Bible studies. It was rewarding when they finally became believers and received Jesus Christ as their Savior. At the time, the Baptistry wasn't finished in our new Southgate Baptist Church. Both wanted to follow the Lord in water baptism, so Clif baptized them in the beautiful Caribbean Sea.

One day, I saw the lady in town, and she said, "Oh, Mrs. Bubar, something terrible has happened to our family."

Clif and I went to their home and learned that their son, A. J. C., had met a woman while in the service, and he had a bad experience with her. Later, after he was out of the service, he and a friend snatched her from her apartment one evening, mistreated her, and murdered her. This was the same son who had served so well in the service and who also had a wife and two children who were living in another land.

I remember after his mother visited her son in prison, she said, "I looked at the palms of his hands. The lines were broken, and they did not run the length of his palms. The broken lines meant he was mixed up, and that was the reason he murdered the girl."

God does not promise that our faith will free us from all discouragements and conflicts. He does promise that the Holy Spirit will give us peace and enable us to weather the storms. He will be with us and comfort us in suffering, even in bitter tragedies, illness, divorce, or death. The Holy Spirit stood with this family to deliver the support they required to cope with the situation.

They later told us, "We have to live on and we are going to live our lives and try to be happy."

How thankful we are that we had a part in introducing them to Jesus Christ and that He helped them through this trying time.

One night, I couldn't sleep, so I got up and wrote a letter to A. J. C., assuring him that Clif and I were praying for him. I enclosed some tracts with the written Word, explaining God's plan of salvation. I also sent him a book.

After he received the letter, he wrote back, saying:

> "I read the verses from the Bible. I prayed and asked God to forgive me and to save me. Whatever my life holds for me now, I have the strength through faith in God to face it. I plan to put my time in jail to good use by using my personal example to help others avoid my mistakes and turn to God. The Bible tells us not to hide our light: though mine may be but a dull glow now, I will be a darker source of light to others rather than remain silent. If I can save just one person from my tragedy, from the fathomless sense of remorse I feel, I will do it. Life is truly priceless, although I am unable to view mine as such. I have been astray for a long time, but now I'm back, perhaps for the first time. If I had your love of God and therefore the strength to attempt to love all my fellow men, the strength to forgive even their most damaging transgressions, I would not be where I am. Thank you again for your book. It is thought provoking and I have found comfort in it. My parents went through an incredible tough time because of the nightmare my life turned into in 1991. I know how important the comfort and support of friends like you were to them, I really don't know how to thank you for extending the same warmth to me. I felt so undeserving of it that it struck me to the

> core. Thank you with all my heart. I know I'm not the only one who thinks fondly of you and prays for you each night. Sincerely, A.J.C."

This letter was written from Death Row, as he waited to be executed in the electric chair.

Late one evening, Clif turned the news on. It showed A. J. C.'s name and a picture of the electric chair; he was to be executed at midnight. We had kept in touch with him by letters over a period of two years and received letters from him. The whole thing was a bittersweet story of victory and hope, despite human failure.

Here's a poem I want to share that was written by him before he passed on into eternity:

Love's Hope

By A. J. C.

Some might say those jailhouse bars confine me,
and were it so my heart would cry for joy.
The awful truth is nothing lies behind them.
An act of vengeance did my life destroy.

All that's left – and now, an only living goal
to do for those whom I must do without.
I'll serve then now (before and after death),
for only in this way can I win out …

I found an interesting article entitled "Life on Death

Row," from the March-April-May 1992 edition of Our Daily Bread; it definitely makes you think:

> "It is appointed for men to die once but after this the judgement." Hebrews 9:27
>
> In this article discussing the U.S. justice system, a newspaper columnist mentioned that nearly two thousand prisoners in America are living on death row – sentenced to die to pay for their crimes.
>
> Think for a moment about what it must be like to live every day under the sentence of death. Imagine the fear that may be on the minds of these people, knowing that they have a date with death.
>
> Yet take that thinking a step further. Although we may feel bad for the inmates on death row, in actuality we all face a similar plight. Each of us lives with death on the horizon.
>
> A fire roars through an apartment building, killing several people. A drunk driver rams head-on into a carload of senior citizens, killing two fine couples. Cancer claims a young mother in the prime of her life. And even if we escape such tragedies, our bodies eventually wear out and we must meet our appointment with death and God.

> We need not get depressed about it, however, if we are ready for God's appointed time for us. By putting our faith in Christ and living for Him, we can face death without the fear of God's judgment. We can live every day to the full, knowing that death will take us on to living with Him.
>
> J. D. B.

Nothing will be able to separate us from the love of God that is in Christ Jesus our Lord.

A Special Musician

To every thing there is season, and a time
to every purpose under the heaven.
—Ecclesiastes 3:1

We really desired a talented piano player for the Southgate Baptist Church, as music is such an important part of a service. So we prayed that God would provide someone who could play beautiful music to prepare hearts for worshipping and to receive the gospel message. Someone referred us to a woman who played dinner music at a charming restaurant on St. Croix. She was a beautiful Christian and a wonderful musician.

We called Carol and made an appointment for her to meet us at our church; when she started to play the piano, tears filled my eyes. Clif was also moved and amazed at her God-given talent. She played so beautifully, and the music rang throughout the church. It was simply amazing; I had to step into another room to dry my tears of joy and thank God for answering our prayer. He provided just what we prayed for.

After talking with Carol, we realized that God had brought her to our church and into our lives for a special reason. She hadn't been attending church. Her parents were deceased but had been Christians, and her father had been a pastor. God, in His loving care, placed her in our church not only so she could play beautiful music but so He could bring a harmony to her life that had been missing.

She had the ability to put beautiful worship music together as God prepared hearts for the messages that Clif brought from God's Word, the Bible. She led and played for the Christmas and Easter Cantatas, which filled the church, and people were so blessed by her gift.

She played the piano faithfully at Southgate Baptist Church for more than two years. Then one day, Gary, a wonderful Christian man who faithfully attended the Southgate Baptist Church, was drawn to her, and a charming romance soon followed. It led to a beautiful wedding Stateside. Clif was unable to perform the ceremony, and we couldn't attend, but we did give them our blessing as they packed up and relocated to the States. We thanked God for loaning her to our church for a strategic season in our growth. It was a beautiful experience to see how God answered prayer and blessed us.

We have since retired and are living in Florida, and Carol and Gary retired to live in Montana. We received a surprise visit one day from them, and it was so exciting to see them talk of God's blessings since we all had been together at the Southgate Baptist Church in St. Croix. How pleasant it was to renew an old friendship in the Lord.

Not long ago, Carol let us know that Gary is now with the Lord. We have such fond memories of him and of our many friends we knew in St. Croix.

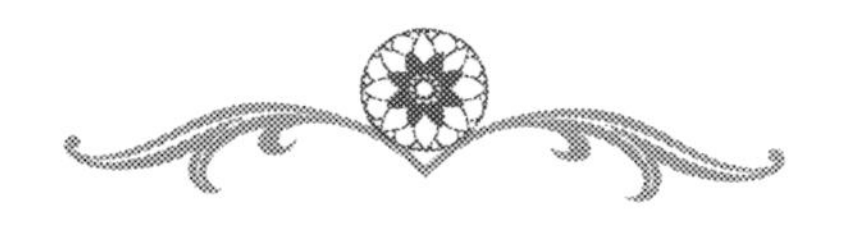

Choices Bring Consequences

It is easier to get into something than to get out of it.
—George Eliot

Do you remember when your mother told you not to do something, and you did it anyway? There were probably times when you were disobedient and severe consequences followed, right?

The following is a tract that I wrote. I titled it "Poor Little Innocent Puppy: A True Story for Boys and Girls."

When I was about four years old, a stray shepherd dog stopped at our house and left six puppies on our back porch. The mama dog disappeared soon after the puppies had their eyes open, so her family was left for us to care for. We soon found homes for five of them, but we kept one of the cute little puppies and named him Jerry.

I will never forget one late afternoon close to dinner time. My mother told me not to go away from the house, but a few minutes later, I saw a neighbor girl, Mary, and forgot what Mom had told me. So off I went with my puppy

Jerry and my friend Mary to the corner store. Mary brought her big bulldog along, as well. We had to cross a main street, where there was heavy traffic since it was evening rush hour. Mary's bulldog ran out into the street in between cars, and little Jerry followed. Suddenly, we heard the squealing of car brakes and saw my puppy lying in the road; he wasn't moving. I ran out and took him in my arms and laid him carefully in the grass beside the road. I ran home crying so hard that I couldn't even tell my mother what happened, but not seeing the puppy with me, she guessed that something had happened to him. She grabbed an old rug and followed me back to the corner, where Jerry lay bleeding and gasping for breath. My mother gently put him in the rug and carried him home in her arms, but Jerry died on the way.

There was no way of knowing that the simple of act of disobedience would lead to a loss of life of something so loving and innocent. There was no way to undo the consequences of disobeying, but in the next thing I tell you, you'll find that someone already paid the consequences for your disobedience.

I tell this story because our disobedience caused the death of someone loving and innocent. Someone had to pay the price for our sins. The Bible tells us, in Romans 3:23, "For all have sinned and come short of the glory of God." A sacrifice had to be made to atone for us, and it required an innocent lamb, the Lamb of God to take the death penalty in our place. Romans 6:23 says, "For the wages of sin is death, but the gift of God is eternal life through Jesus Christ our Lord." Jesus is the Lamb of God, and He loved us so much that He died a cruel death on the cross to pay the price to redeem us from sin. He died in our place and took the punishment that we deserved for our sins. He did this so that God would forgive us and not punish us. For God so loved the world.

Jesus wants us to be happy and to live forever with Him in heaven. He is preparing a place for us in heaven, where it will be wonderful and where there is no sin, sickness, or sadness. It is a perfect place. God is there. We did not deserve to go this place, but Jesus took our punishment for sin and paid the price in full with His sacrifice on the cross, making a way for us to come home to our heavenly Father.

Jesus said, "Come unto me" (Matthew 11:28).

Jesus said, "I am the way" (John 14:6).

"Suffer the little children to come unto me" (Mark 10:14).

"Choose ye this day whom ye will serve" (Joshua 24:15).

Have you chosen to serve God? Have you prayed and asked Jesus to forgive you and to take away your sin? If not, then today is the day for you to make things right with God, based on what Jesus already did on the cross for you.

My Decision

I now believe "For God so loved the world, that he gave his only begotten Son, that whosoever believeth in him should not perish, but have everlasting life." John 3:16

"Whosoever" (your name here)

____

My Prayer

Dear Jesus, right now I ask you to come into my heart and take away all of my sins. I thank you for dying on the cross in my place. Help me to live a new life every day as I read my Bible and obey it. Fill my life with your Holy Spirit that other people will be able to see you living in me. Prepare me here on earth for that wonderful Home up in heaven that is for all people who love God and accept His Son. These things I ask in Jesus's name. Amen.

My Prayer

Dear Jesus, right now I ask you to come into my heart and take away my sins. I thank you for dying on the cross in my place. Please help me to live a new life every day. Please help me to read my Bible and obey it. Fill my life with your Holy Spirit so that other people will be able to see you living in me. Prepare me here on earth for that wonderful home in heaven that is for all people who love God and accept His Son Jesus as their Savior. These things I ask in Jesus's name. Thank you. Amen!

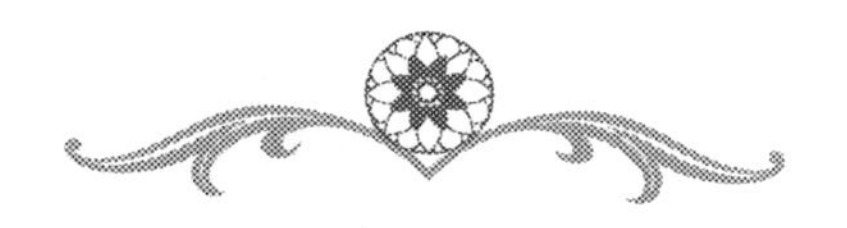

The Adventure of Dave and Jean Mueller through Hurricane Hugo

By Jean Mueller

Hurricane warnings were a normal part of summer life for those living on islands in the Caribbean. It's like threats of tornadoes and blizzards for people living in the Midwest. The summer of 1989 had already had two major warnings: Hurricanes Dean and Gabrielle. A major hurricane had not hit the Virgin Islands since 1928, so the large majority of residents on St. Croix had no first-hand experience.

Dave and Jean had been living on St. Croix for eight months, having come to assist the Bubars in the work at Southgate Baptist Church. They were weary from the enormous job of building the church in heat and humidity of the past two years and were taking several weeks furlough in the States.

Days found the temperature in the nineties and the humidity averaging 95 percent, with very little breeze. Fans went day and night with no air conditioning. The warnings of Hurricane Hugo were being announced on the radio, and the winds were picking up. We tracked the course on a map; knowing that we were at 16 and 64 degrees, an air of concern prevailed. The grocery store was packed, with not a shopping cart available. All bottled water was gone and flashlights, batteries, canned food, and bread had all been snatched up like there would be no more stores.

We secured everything at the church. I put an "X" with wide tape on the windows on all eight sides of the building, hoping they would not shatter. Dave used strong wire to secure an overhang entrance roof to concrete columns, as suggested by Clif in a last-minute phone call the night before. Then we took care of things around the house. Anything loose was put inside. I called our daughter, Sally, and told her we would be fine as we were going to the Bubars' house. It seemed much safer than the wood frame structure that we were in. The wind was stronger than usual all night. Palm trees were bending over.

We made ourselves comfortable in Kerwin's room. He was the most recent of many for which the Bubars have provided shelter for in the small prophet's chamber. Dave carefully removed the panel forming a wall between Kerwin's room and the adjoining apartment. He did not want to damage the wall or the board. The wind was so strong, we were forced to close the louvers on the door, the only window. It was very closed up and dark. The electricity would surely go off, as it did frequently throughout the year.

The radio carried only warnings of a "Class 4" hurricane and offered continuous information of what should be done to protect life and property. Shelters were open to anyone who felt that their home was not safe or who did not want to stay alone. Boats had been taken to the more secure inlets and bays or brought onto land. Large boats were anchored farther out at sea, away from piers or reefs. Strong warnings were given to those who lived on their boats.

The power had gone off at two in the afternoon, so for our evening meal, we ate generously of refrigerated food, as our ice supply was already thawing. At 7:30 p.m., we went to bed thinking it might be a long night. We had no idea how long a night it would be. Dave went right to sleep as usual, but my eyes would not shut. I heard strange noises, banging, creaking, and cracking. I would frequently awaken Dave and suggest that we open or close the louvers on windows, move something, or check something else. Toady, LeEllen's poodle, was in bed with us. Cherokee, their Doberman, was lying right beside us, both scared and trembling. I had never seen Cherokee in the house before.

After what seemed like forever, I shined the flashlight on my watch: 1 a.m. And we wondered if the eye of the storm would pass over. This was to bring a brief calm, after which the winds would come from the north instead of the present south and east. It would also lead us to believe that the storm was half over. Dave sensed possible danger with the sounds of many things crashing all around outside, so we slipped into our shorts and t-shirts. The bedroom door rattled constantly, and Dave decided to try to have it open, though that allowed more noise and wind into the bedroom. As he did, terrible crashing noises made him realize the slats of the louvered windows and the screens had blasted into the kitchen and living room. At the same time, I could see lightning flashing through holes in the ceilings of the bedroom that we were in, as well as Kerwin's bed; we had put large trash bags on it to keep the leaking roof from harming the mattress. Now the bed was covered with rafters and roof boards.

No place appeared safe, so we went into a small hallway to decide our next move and to pray. We had already prayed many times for safety and wisdom, and now we needed both. Lightning continued to flash through the enlarging holes, as rain and more of the roof poured in. The battery-powered lantern had been knocked over and would not work, and we could not find the flashlight or the radio that had been placed carefully by our bed. The bathtub seemed as safe as any place, with concrete walls on three sides of it, and the bathroom roof was still on. We got into the tub, holding the shelf board and pillows around our heads for protection from flying debris. Toady was right there with us, Cherokee was next to us, and we knew the Lord was with us.

As we crouched together in the tub, we clutched each other, our shelf boards, and pillows. We affirmed our great love for each other and the thankfulness that we had for our thirty-five years together. We prayed for our four children, their spouses, and our four grandchildren. We admitted to God that we would love to see each of them again. Indeed, we were ready to go to heaven, but this seemed like a terrible way to die. Dave cried out to the Lord, pleading for safety and for Him to quiet the winds. I was almost speechless, a reversal of our usual roles.

The extremely low air pressure made our mouths and throats parched, and our ears ached like we were in a rapidly descending airplane. We wished we were. Dave groped around and found a jug of water, which helped both problems. He also found our shoes. This was a calmer time, as the eye had probably passed over us; it was hard to tell. The storm had stalled, traveling only at 6 mph.

As winds up to 200 mph continued on and on, more roofing crashed in the bedrooms, and rain and lightning were almost constant. The full moon shone between and around the clouds. The TV antenna finally quit banging – it must be down now. Strips of wood hammered to be free. The door of the bathroom blew shut, then open, then banged shut again and again. At last it crashed open, into the hallway: the wrong way. Now it was swinging from just one hinge, into the bathroom, then back into the hall.

Dave ripped the door from its final hinge and wedged it at an angle between the walls surrounding the bathtub. Together, we squeezed under it, now able to use our pillows to help make us more comfortable with Toady, the poodle, still trembling on my lap. Dave continued praying, thanking the Lord for providing this means of security as things continued to fly in and out of the house. With no door now, the wind swept freely through the bedroom. Thankfully, the slats were still in that window, though the screen had blown in.

We were exhausted and felt we had done all that we could to provide for our safety, so we again committed ourselves to God's perfect plan. I continued to pray silently. Would anyone find us if we were trapped in this crashed-in home? Does Jesus care?

"Does Jesus care when my heart is pained too deeply for mirth and song, as the burdens press and the cares distress, and the way grows weary and long? Does Jesus care when I've said goodbye to the dearest on earth to me, and my sad heart aches till it nearly breaks – it is ought to him, does He see? Oh yes! He cares! I know He cares! His heart is touched with my grief. When the days are weary and the long night dreary, I know my Savior cares!"

With complete trust in knowing God was still in control, we slumped into the bathtub and got as comfortable as we could. We were together, and I hinted to the Lord that I preferred we remain that way, dead or alive. A restful peace came over us, even while the sounds of crashing and crackling continued in the relentless winds.

Apparently, we had dozed off as we realized the first rays of light were coming through the holes in the roof. Unbending our cramped legs and climbing out of the bathtub, we could hear and feel that the wind had subsided considerably. The mess inside the Bubars' house was everywhere, with rain continuing to fall into the bedroom and blow into the now window-less living area.

Looking outside, we soon learned the source of much of the problem: The frail, wooden pre-fab house next door, used as a kindergarten, had blown apart, with most of it flying into the Bubars' yard. Apparently roof trusses had catapulted onto and over our roof, with some coming through. Others were scattered all about the yard, with 4 x 8 roof boards, shingles still attached and pink insulation covering everything. One wall of the school was still standing, an open cupboard containing paper and supplies looking forlorn. The devastation to the trees and the bushes was beyond belief or description. Everywhere we looked, trees were down, uprooted, or broken off in part or whole. Fronds from palm trees mixed with broken-off branches were everywhere.

In shoes soaked from sloshing through water in the house, we wandered in the rain around the yard. Friends from church walked by and begin telling how they survived the long night. Neighbors Williams and Ivan were walking from house to house to see if everyone was safe. Both of their own roofs had blown off. With trees and bushes all down, we could see the cupola on Southgate Baptist Church. Over and over, we thanked God and praised Him for preserving our lives; we had not realized how bad it really had been. We were thankful it occurred at night, so we could not see the destruction happening or be tempted to go outside for any reason.

We scooped some of the water off of the floor of the living room; picked up the window slats, roof boards, and tree limbs that had blown into the house; and then set off to check on the church. Thankfully, the rain subsided at times, but walking on the road was difficult, as we had to climb over and around fallen trees, branches, and telephone poles. Williams and Ivan were continuing their mission and helped us make our way through brush and rubble and rain-swollen gullies. Ivan lifted me across a difficult ditch.

It was exciting to see the Southgate Baptist Church standing firm on the hillside. A closer look revealed many shingles off the roof, three broken windows, and water soaking the large expanse of beautiful green carpet; rain was pouring onto the pulpit, communion table, piano, organ, and pews. The cupola had only three of the eight glass panels left in, the very heavy picnic table was blown away, the small porch roof that David had secured to the concrete pillars was gone, and the pillars had blown over.

Several people came to rest on the benches on the church patio. The stories became familiar: "Our roof and belongings are gone but thank God that we are alive." Ivan's wife and children joined others resting on the bench; eleven of them had huddled in a closet and now she was looking for anything that was dry for them that night. She walked with us to our house.

By now, we had seen so much destruction that we felt prepared to find everything of ours blown away or in a pile of rubble. I said, "David, I think I can see the red roof." We could certainly see much more than before the storm, now that there were no trees or bushes to block the view. Indeed, the red roof was there, and we quickly checked on a neighbor living alone and then went up to our apartment. Two windows on opposite walls had blown in. The refrigerator had blown over in the middle of the floor, belongings strewn everywhere. Two sheet rock panels were dangling over our bed, with insulation falling all around. It was certainly better than most. With tears of praise flowing, we continued to thank God.

We walked and later drove to as many of our church friends as we could, sometimes bringing food or water but mostly just to listen. Our immediate task was to help with temporary roofing, getting standing water out, as well as starting to dry out furnishings in homes as well as the church.

Rains continued for several days, keeping our private brooks filled and overflowing with water for washing and flushing. Thankfully, our source of good water was intact. We worked from sunup to sundown to help friends try to keep the rain out and clean up. It seemed like a losing battle at church, as the tarps Dave and the other men put on the roof could not cover all the holes. He covered Bubars' roof the best that he could with boards found in the yard, plus tarps. In one home, I helped a friend sort through the rubble of all her china, glassware, and figurines. We found one piece whole from her set for twelve. I later cleaned out refrigerators that had been closed for two and three weeks. Family pictures, diplomas, Christmas decorations, and legal papers were soaked or blown away. One cannot fathom the heartbreak as we listened to story after story of loss and destruction.

With our radio soaked, our only information came via car radio from the station on St. Thomas. We heard of a few ham radio operators and finally met a boat leaving for St. Thomas and gave out cards to several folks, asking them to contact the BGC and also our children. We had no idea if anyone off the islands even knew we had a problem.

Friends we met told us the stores had all been looted; we saw one small grocery store being cleaned out. We became concerned as our food supply was dwindling, with no refrigeration. I wrote in my journal, "We had the last two slices of bread tonight, with peanut butter and jelly, as usual. We ate by the light of only one candle and couldn't see if the bread was moldy."

We talked with the pastors of other BGC churches on St. Croix. The Sunny Isle Church lost a lot of windows, but Pastor Butler's family was safe and secure in their new parsonage. Pastors Woods, Rogers, Bubar, and Benjamin all received damage to their homes. The roof was off over the Altona Church office. The roofs were gone from the

Frederiksted Baptist Church and Calvary Baptist Church. Pastor Navarro lost the roof of his home, but the Spanish church was undamaged. Each had a story to tell about the long night for their family and the folks in their churches.

By the end of the week, we were weary with sore arms, legs, and backs. My fingernails were worn to nubbins. We were getting furniture dried out, put carpets and bedding out to dry, and got water off the floor. We were happy to see Clif and his son, Mark, arrive with the generator that they brought, as many generators had come up missing. A generator meant that we could cool down the refrigerator some, have a light on in the evening, and pump up water. A week after Hugo, we had our first showers. Never complain about unheated water.

Clif also brought some food, batteries, and plastic for roofs. All was put to good use immediately. Each evening, though exhausted, Clif and Mark went to the homes of fellow pastors, neighbors, and others and hooked up the generator to their water pumps so that they could have a supply of water. A "cup of cold water" in Christ's name has never had more meaning.

The Sunday following the hurricane, we met for an informal service on the gazebo at the church. The carpet inside the church had water standing on it. David shared passages from the Psalms; hymns were sung that also reminded us of God's everlasting love and protection for us. Many shared stories, thanking God that they were still alive and their renewed thankfulness for the gift of eternal life, which cannot be taken from us. A spirit of thanks and praise to the Lord prevailed.

A week later, however, a feeling of despair set in, as people were physically weary and realizing the immense rebuilding task ahead. Food supplies were short, and there was almost no communication system. One thousand soldiers had arrived to restore and maintain order, army vehicles were everywhere, and planes and helicopters flew overhead constantly. It looked and felt like a war zone. One man left the island because it reminded him too much of Vietnam, and another neighbor committed suicide.

At last, telephone centers were set up, with long lines of people waiting for their five-minute allotment. Frustration mounted. About the tenth day, the Red Cross began the task of distributing huge quantities of food brought over by the US government. The military assisted by hauling it to various sites; later, the Southgate Church became a distribution center. Dave and I assisted in that program. At first only pork, red beans, and orange juice were given out, and the people soon mumbled. Quite a variety of canned and packaged food arrived later.

LeEllen and Joan Bubar arrived in two weeks, and we had a great time of celebration in seeing them again. However, walking through their home and seeing over thirty years' of belongings soaking up water was very depressing. Though she had been told of the destruction, seeing it was much worse. We cried with and for them. LeEllen had gathered together a great amount of supplies as well as another generator. She even brought fresh meat and frozen orange juice. Funds had been sent from Baptist World Relief for her to use.

A few days later, there was much excitement as a DC3 plane from Jungle Aviation and Radio Service (JAARS) landed on St. Croix. Aubrey Husky and Rollow Entz accompanied the four pilots and delivered hundreds of pounds of supplies. To each of the BGC pastors, we brought a generator, a propane stove, and a crate filled with food, clothes, flashlights, batteries, tire repair kits – more things than one can imagine. Some lost a great deal, and wives were happy to have new towels, clothes, and other lovely things from the BGC Missionary Boutique.

The government agencies and the Red Cross helped with shelter, food, and basic human needs, including mental health. Lives became more settled and greatly encouraged as the trees and bushes begin to be covered with green leaves again.

Two weeks post-Hugo, in 1989, Dave and Jean Mueller left St. Croix as crews from BGC churches and others were arriving to start the massive task of rebuilding. God graciously spared the lives of almost fifty thousand residents on St. Croix, and we believe that He has a perfect plan for each one of them. Our continued prayer is that many, many will be thankful for physical life and come to joy enjoy eternal Life.

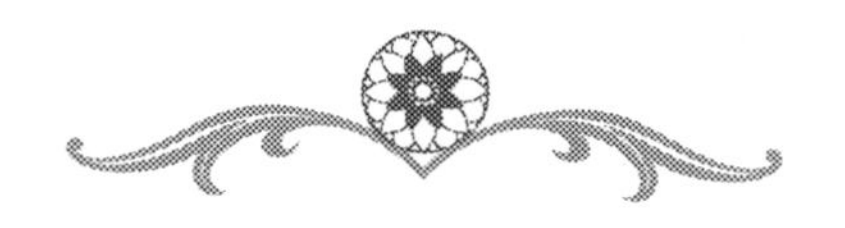

David R. Mueller's Home Going

On June 13, 2009, a memorial celebration service was held at the Penney Memorial Church in Jacksonville, Florida. Dave R. Mueller had moved to the Penny Retirement Community in Jacksonville several months before his home going.

David and Jean Mueller found a great enjoyment serving the Lord. They served on short-term missions, including time in the United States in Florida, in Trinidad, in St. Croix in the US Virgin islands, and in Brazil and in Cebu, Philippines. The Muellers were a blessing to many people.

Dare to say yes to God. They did.

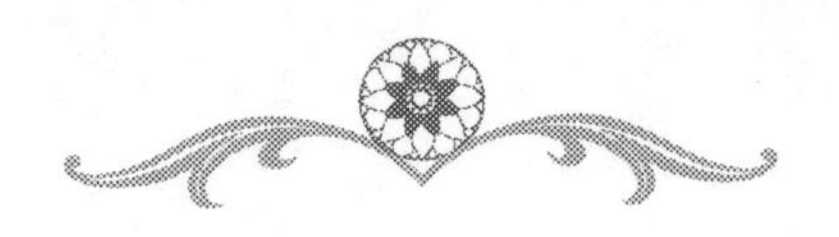

Mission Accomplished

I have fought the good fight, I have finished
the race, I have kept the faith.
—2 Timothy 4:7

Clif and I are people who have a vision, commit to the vision, labor for the vision, bring it to fruition, and then take great joy as we say a very satisfying phrase: "Mission Accomplished!" I like the saying so much I might have it put under my name on my tombstone, should I go on to my reward before our Lord's return. Even though Clif and I say, "Mission Accomplished," to mark the end of a chapter, we find that simply means we're about to begin another. It's so exciting when you dare to say yes and keep saying yes to the Lord.

Perhaps there is no such thing as "retirement" with the Lord, only "re-fire-ment." We're firing up to do more work as God leads because, haven't you noticed, the fields are white unto harvest and the laborers are few? We're praying God sends laborers (you) into the harvest. No one needs to be spiritually unemployed. God's got a purpose and a plan for all of us, and there's plenty of work to be done. We're all needed in the Kingdom of God.

I titled this chapter "Mission Accomplished" because I want to share with you the letter that Clif and I wrote to the last church we built on St. Croix. It's important to know God's timing, not only when to begin something but also when to move on to His next assignment.

Here's our "Mission Accomplished!" letter:

August 25, 1992

Dear friends,

"There is a time to be born, and a time to die: a time to plant, and a time to pluck up." Ecclesiastes 3:2

We've had the privilege of ministering for 36 years on St. Croix. It's been rewarding to serve him these years. When we came to St. Croix in 1956, there were no Baptist churches. We've had the privilege of building and establishing several Baptist churches throughout the island of St. Croix from Frederiksted to Christiansted. We've also helped other missionaries on other islands in the Caribbean. Praise the Lord for those who have accepted Christ in these churches. And more important, these churches will continue to be a lighthouse in preaching the Word until Christ returns.

We sense the timing to be right here for a vital period of ministry and growth. Praise the Lord! Five people followed the Lord in the waters of baptism this past Sunday.

But in seeking God's will for our lives at this time, we feel ... MISSION ACCOMPLISHED! After much prayer and thought, we feel it is time for us to resign from the Southgate Baptist Church where we are now ministering. We plan to continue here until a new pastor is located for the Church. Please join us in prayer that God will direct another pastor to Southgate.

Let us explain why we feel this is the time to leave St. Croix, and what we mean by "Mission Accomplished." Although there is still much to be done for God here, there are now many churches taking up that mission. And now we pray God will let us continue our vision and mission of helping to establish Baptist churches but in a different place.

As our faithful supporters, we wanted to tell you personally that:
1) We are not retiring.
2) We plan to resume our home missions ministry in the Florida Baptist Conference, still under the Baptist General Conference as home missionaries.

These transition weeks are bringing mixed emotions, leaving an island where we have lived most of our lives, where our son and our grandson were born, where we have loved and enjoyed working with the people of St. Croix (planting churches).

The packing and moving takes our thoughts back to our graduation days at college, the anxiety and the excitement of packing up barrels and coming to an island we knew little about ... this time returning to the States, where we feel almost foreign.

To our dear friends who have encouraged, prayed, and supported us these 36 years on St. Croix, we want to say thank you from the bottom of our hearts. We couldn't have come this far without you, and we will continue to need and appreciate your support and prayers in our new location of service.

In Christian love,
Clif and LeEllen

Clif and LeEllen Bubar
Your Missionaries

With God's help, we founded the first Baptist church on St. Croix and built and pastored a total of three Baptist churches during our thirty-six years there. God enabled us to build strong churches, both the structures and the congregations. When we left a church to build another, it was only after the church's mortgage was paid in full, the church was full, and there was money in their account. To God be all the glory. And many thanks to all that He sent to share the labor and in his reward.

We found some pictures of some of the folks who came to work with us building churches on St. Croix. Some pictures haven't been located, but God keeps an account. Those we found are individual pictures I've put on several pages. Some folks came from the States and stayed two weeks, some a couple of months; some men came from Sunny Isle Baptist Church Saturdays to help Southgate Baptist Church.

Frederiksted Baptist Church, St. Croix

Sunny Isle Baptist Church, St. Croix

Southgate Baptist Church, St. Croix

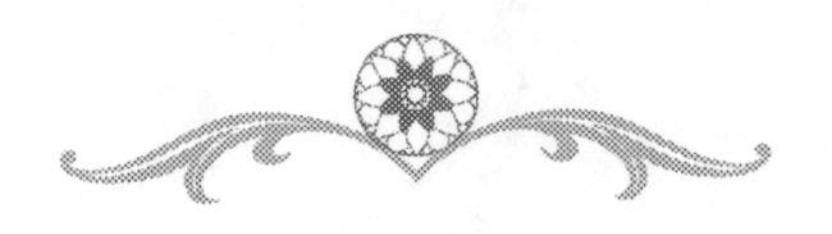

The Elinor

A stately three-mast schooner built as a Caribbean cargo ship. It was a beautiful funeral service, led by their pastor from Pennsylvania and Pastor Clif Bubar of the South Gate Baptist Church, St. Croix, V.I. John and Dottie were blessings at the S.G.B. Church. John offered his backhoe to be used at the Southgate Baptist Church. Dottie was so talented with a solo voice and handmade flower talent, decorating the Southgate Church with the unique seafoam Caribbean colors, most beautiful. Thank you, Dottie and John. John is in his heavenly home; what a day that will be when we all join together up there.

The Elinor

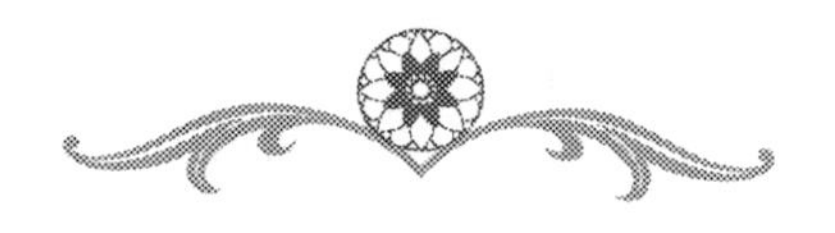

Building Churches

A brief word about my husband, Clifford Bubar. He was born and grew up in Maine. He lived on a farm where his father had cows and a few other farm animals. His father also had a logging business, cutting trees in large forests and hauling them to the log mill or to a paper mill. Clif never dreamed that someday he would build Baptist churches in the Caribbean or that he would build anything larger than a dog house or a chicken coop.

Why a Baptist church? When we arrived on St. Croix in 1956, there were no Baptist churches on the island. We were Baptist and saw the need for a Baptist believing church.

We give thanks for the Baptist General Conference and the many BGC churches that prayed and supported us and loaned the money for the churches that were built and those people who came out and helped from those churches.

How did we do it? An elderly couple who we had a Bible studies with accepted Jesus Christ as their Savior. They also saw the need for a Baptist church. We couldn't afford to buy land or hire a contractor to build it. But God made a way. God provided the land by Mr. and Mrs. Ludvig Johansson, Sr. Missionary Clif Bubar was the church builder. With a goal in mind and trust in God, he helped us reach the goal. God's Word and prayer was the strength of our lives. It overcame doubts and gave victory in reaching the goal.

Plans were drawn up for Sunny Isle Baptist Church. Clif was studying pages of plans when Dad Lyons, my father, saw the stack of papers.

Dad said, "Clif, who's going to build this church?"

Clif said, "We are, Dad."

Dad had helped Clif build the Frederiksted Baptist Church, the first Baptist church on St. Croix. It was built with eight-inch concrete blocks, a simple straight block structured building, quite different to this hyperbolic paraboloid design. Dad could hardly pronounce the name, hyperbolic paraboloid, let alone entertain the thought of helping Clif build a complicated-looking building.

The days ahead were getting some of the groundwork started; there were days Clif used the pick and shovel, digging the footings and foundation. The sun was beating down, and the days were scorching hot. Clif could wring the perspiration out of his shirt it was so hot, as sweat rolled down his red, sunburned face. It seemed like this job would never end, and many of the same days followed.

I didn't know then about the little talk Clif had with the Lord as he shoveled and used a pickax to dig the dirt footings. "Lord, why am I doing this? When will it ever get done? I need help and strength to go on with this project." After his talk with the Lord and some lunch, Clif continued on with the pick and shovel, digging where he left off, but with an added spark of faith and a power surge of courage to go on. The project God called Clif to do continued on. Sometimes unexpected obstacles became a bump in the road to test our faith. But we knew God would continue to help us to the finished line.

Clif had labored hard and long hours, and we were encouraged over his progress. By this time, the church was about three-quarters finished. An 80-by-80 concrete floor had been poured. The white hypalon roof towered tall. The high ceiling was of structured curves of beautiful cypress wood. There stood a huge building, incomplete, no outside walls, windows, or doors, just a tall, open building.

Reverend Gordon Anderson from BGC, our mission board, visited us. We were happy to have Gordon and his wife, Ethel Anderson. The first thing we wanted them to see was the progress on the new church building, the Sunny Isle Baptist Church. We were so thrilled that God had given property for a second Baptist church. Clif and Gordon stepped into the huge building, with no doors, windows, or sides completed.

Gordon looked up as his eyes scanned the huge, empty building. He said, "Clif, are you sure you're not building this church too big?"

That was the first time Cliff had given that idea a thought. It never crossed his mind until someone with insight brought it to mind. Clif had a vision and a goal and kept his eyes on God. Everyone doesn't have the same vision.

And guess what? Clif finished the church, it was paid off, the mortgage was burned, and there was money in the bank when we left to build the third church. Praise God.

The Johansens gave property to plant a beautiful third Baptist church in the area of Estate Southgate, east of Christiansted town. It was a beautiful location for a church, on a paved road traveled by islanders, visitors, and tourists. One day, a contractor stopped by the property; he told Clif he liked the area and view and would like to trade some of his land for the Southgate property to build houses.

"A church shouldn't be sitting on that kind of property," he commented.

Clif told him, "God gave the property to build a Baptist church at the east end of the island, where there were no Baptist churches. A beautiful church on the side of the hill would draw islanders and visitors to hear the gospel message in song and word."

Clearing the land began. Sonny Johansen used his heavy equipment to clear and level an area for the church. Rain water being the main water supply on St. Croix, a huge hole was dug where a large concrete cistern would be built. Clif, Romesh, and Scot Green labored tying steel rods for the floor and walls of the cistern. Plywood was placed for forms, and concrete was poured for the 32,000-gallon water cistern. The costly cistern was in the ground before the church floor could be poured.

An octagon church was planted on the hillside overlooking a beautiful, gorgeous view of the Caribbean Sea. Arch windows surrounded the eight-sided building in keeping with the Danish décor of the island and to catch the Caribbean trade winds throughout the building. Bill Anderson of Bethel Baptist Church of Bradenton, Florida, drew the church plans. When it was time to build the arch window frames, God provided a carpenter from the state of Oregon. An elderly couple, Albert and Judy Stroh, labored together on the frame arches. Both must be looking down from Glory now with praise and thanks to the Lord for the part they had in helping to plant the Southgate Baptist Church before graduating to their heavenly home.

Some men came from the Sunny Isle Baptist Church on Saturdays to help on the foundations of the Southgate Baptist Church. The DeLeons were faithful cooking food most Saturdays. During the week, Tony helped Clif on the building; when the huge church floor was poured, he helped with the concrete. Some men came from Stateside BGC churches to help on the building. Dave and Elsa Weborg from Wisconsin were a tremendous help on the church and on our house. Hurricane Hugo took some of our house roof with high winds. Bill and Lu Anderson from Bethel Baptist Church in Bradenton and Fran Nelson from Chicago brought food and helped on the church. Bill Anderson and his son donated the beautiful chandeliers and electrical materials for the church. Bill did the electrical work. Bud and Ginny Lyons were visiting us at the time; Bud helped run wires. Perry Galusha came for several months and was a tremendous help. Clif and Perry worked together building, planting the church. Perry could carry two fifty-pound bags of cement as if they were five pounds of sugar. By the way, after Perry met Sandy, Sonny Johansen's daughter, wedding bells rang out on St. Croix, as Clif married them.

John and Dottie Dessolet from Pennsylvania were a tremendous help to the church. John had a backhoe and used it around the church property. Dottie's touch of color décor in the church and her lovely voice of music were a blessing to the church. Mr. Rowan's heavy equipment company on St. Croix donated a crane. Mr. Strong worked for the company and donated his time to operate the crane, putting the steel frame up. Other short-term helpers came from Canada. A youth group came to work on the church from Bethel Baptist Church in Bradenton, with Pastor Don and Peggy Windmiller.

One day, I watched a man with rough, crude hands hammer, chip, and face rocks, stacking one rock on top of another and slapping mortar in between the rocks. The church arched windows would sit on the rock wall and be part of the church building. Clif and I had previously picked these beige colored rocks, called bones of the earth, from dirt rock piles in neighborhoods where cistern holes had been dug. First, we asked the owner if they had use for the rocks. If not, would they mind if we picked them up and loaded them into our pickup truck for the new church building at Southgate? Most people were glad to get rid of them, not realizing the beauty and value of the hand-picked rock. We knew. It not only was beautiful rock and added to the beauty of the church, but it saved us from buying blocks for the walls around the church that could have added up to several thousand dollars.

Guess what? The man I had been watching lay the stone wall didn't show up for several days. We found out that he was called back to the job he was working on at a condominium. So I put on a pair of gloves, found a chipping hammer, and started to work on the wall where the man had left off. That wall was about three and a half feet high and ran the entire length of the building. It's the side of the church where the church organ sits. I did several feet along that area, and the man came back.

I thought he might be upset with the rock I had laid, but he said, "Good job!"

Well, he finished that wall and left for good. The back of the Baptistery needed to be done yet.

I said, "Clif what are we going to do?"

Guess what? Clif said, "You're going to do it."

I was still young then and could climb, so why not? Sonny reminded us of the time I climbed up the steep rocky hill behind the church and came tumbling down. He said Clif turned to look but was busy and kept doing what he was doing, so he guessed no one got hurt.

Anyway, the Baptistery rock wall became LeEllen's job. Clif mixed the cement mortar and made a scaffold for me to stand on in the Baptistery. He worked on another project for the church while I chipped and faced rock and laid rock on the wall in the Baptistery. It was a wall about ten feet high and six feet wide. And seventeen years later, the Baptistery wall is still holding and standing strong, and people are following the Lord in the waters of Baptism.

Southgate Baptist Church was the third Baptist church we built on St. Croix. It was a steel frame building. Clif ordered the steel from Puerto Rico.

It was a new adventure for Clif, for us, and a great undertaking and a step of faith. But not for God; our Lord knew that it would be "Mission Accomplished."

I am sure you realize these churches didn't just pop into existence, or an expensive contractor and we charged and paid later, oh No ... No ... No! As missionaries, we look to win people to the Lord. We knocked on doors, going door-to-door; we looked to buy property and found ways to save money on building materials. Clif was thrifty. We didn't have money; we went to the bank to borrow money. The first church we built, we went to the bank in

Frederiksted to borrow money. The bank manager told Clif (the builder) to borrow money, he would have to have a member in the church must be able to pay off the loan in full.

Churches came into existence due to the Baptist General Conference at that time, and many individuals had a vital part to making this project come to pass. Some said I'll give, and some said I'll pray. Some said we will go, including us. Back in the sixties, mission projects were not as popular as they are now, and when we built the South Gate Baptist Church, it seemed more people were moved to fly to mission fields to help with hands on mission building projects. However God had a plan that worked, we had our health, strength, and encouragement to see our vision fulfilled, and it was. We call it Mission Accomplished! Thank you, thank you, Lord.

Many of you won't be able to go to a mission field far away but you can go by traveling on your knees in prayer for both those who labor and those who are lost.

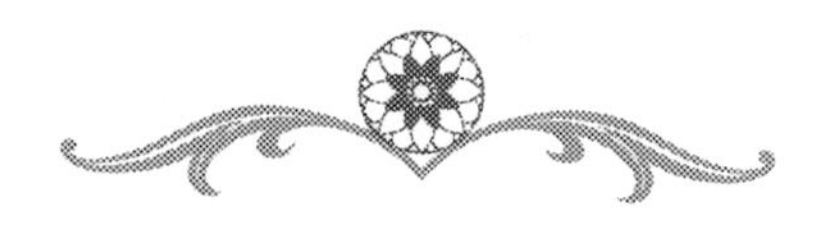

Traveling on My Knees

Last night, I took a journey to a land across the seas.
I did not take a ship or a plane, I traveled on my knees.
I saw so many people there, in bondage to their sin,
and Jesus told me I should go, for
there were souls to win.
But I said, "Jesus, I can't go to a land across the seas."
He quickly answered, "Yes, you can,
by traveling on your knees."
And so I did, I knelt to pray, took off some hours of ease,
and with my Savior by my side, I traveled on my knees.
And as I prayed, I saw souls saved, I
saw twisted persons healed.
I saw God's work of strength through
laborers in the field.
I said, "Yes, Lord, I'll take the job,
your heart I want to please.
I'll heed your call, I'll quickly go by
traveling on my knees."

—Unknown

Missionary Stories

Exciting stories for Christian workers looking for true stories for youth meetings, Sunday schools, youth groups, Vacation Bible schools, youth camps, and adult meeting groups. For sermon illustrations in the church, a golden opportunity to share true missionary stories with the young, also with seniors. These true stories used in churches and Bible youth camps will encourage hearts.

Read about the exciting, adventurous life of the Bubars on the island of St. Croix. Becoming missionaries in the Caribbean was like landing in a different world. They drove on the left side of the road, along with donkeys and donkey carts; there were fewer cars back then in 1956. It all started in their early twenties when they were members of the Bethel Baptist Church in Bradenton, Florida. They attended Trinity College in Clearwater, Florida; after receiving their four-year BA degrees, they answered God's call and dared to say yes.

These true short stories will inspire you to read about those who dared to say, "Yes, God." It was and is our Father's desire to bless. God's compassion for people never ends. On this missionary couple's journey, God spoke to their hearts in a missionary service. Reverend Don Luttrell brought a message on missions (why should some people hear the gospel story twice, when some people haven't heard the story once); it touched and moved their hearts.

Maybe reading this book will inspire you to say "Yes, God." If so, it will be worth the hours of prayer and work put forth on *Dare to Say, Yes God*. We did.

Clif and LeEllen Bubar

True Short Stories

Here read some exciting stories

Urgent Advice by Nadyne, LeEllen's Sister (missionary to Japan)

Our World: The Island of St. Croix

Fisherman Go Where the Fish Are

A Boyhood Dream

A Dangerous Encounter

Searching Everywhere

The Old Man Who Lived in Tree

Stories and Pictures of Clif and LeEllen

Mission Accomplished

Printed in the United States
By Bookmasters